The WICKETT SISTERS
In Time

The Wickett Sisters
In Time

STEPHEN HOUSER

A Novel by Stephen Houser

Copyright © 2020 by Stephen Houser

Lionel A Blanchard, Publisher

All rights reserved. No part of this publication may be reproduced, stored in a retrieval system, or transmitted, in any form or by any means, electronic, mechanical, photocopying, recording, or otherwise, without the prior written permission of the author.

This is a work of fiction. Names, characters, places, and incidents either are the product of the author's imagination or are used fictitiously.
Any resemblance to actual persons, living or dead, events, or locales is entirely coincidental.

First Printing

Hardcover ISBN: 978-1-7335858-3-5
Softcover ISBN: 978-0-9972984-4-4

Cover Art and Design by Vincent Chong

Printed in the United States of America

*With love and appreciation,
this Wickett sisters story is dedicated
to the two great actresses who crossed my path
and inspired these characters.*

Jean Smart and Meryl Streep

CHAPTER ONE

The man walked alone in the shadows of New Babylon's streets. He was dressed in a black tuxedo, a black cape with a scarlet lining, and a black top hat. He could have been a gentleman returning home from the opera. But he was not. He was a beast looking for prey.

A Sekhmet demon was standing on the corner. She had long bare legs and a thong covering her female parts. Her breasts were naked and she had the head of a lioness. Sekhmet females had once been worshipped as goddesses in ancient Egypt. Now they were paid for sex in dark alleys.

The Beau Brummel walked up to the Sekhmet and looked into her golden eyes.

"You are quite a lovely creature," he said.

"But my face is probably not what you're interested in, is it?" the streetwalker asked and grinned lasciviously.

The gentleman smiled, aroused.

"A pretty face is always a plus," he replied. "But I actually do have a thing for long, perfect necks. Perhaps you'd step into that quiet place with me?" He nodded toward an unlit alley a few steps away. In its dark confines, the gentleman drew close. The prostitute pulled back.

"Let's see your money before getting all fresh, mister," she demanded.

The gentleman reached toward his belt and before the Sekhmet knew what had happened, he'd put an opened barber's blade against her throat.

"Oh, God," the Sekhmet moaned. "What are you doing?"

"Enjoying my particular pleasure, sweet thing," the man answered. He could feel the Sekhmet quiver with fear. "What is your name?"

"Inhapi," she said trying to control her terror. "What do you want from me?"

The man cut deeply across her throat. Without a sound the Sekhmet fell to her knees clutching her neck. Blood spurted over her hands and ran down her bare breasts. The man lifted his shoe and pushed the Sekhmet onto her back. She looked at him, eyes half-closed, barely conscious as the blood gushed out of her body.

"Who are you?" she gasped.

The man gazed at her, but did not answer.

"What is your name?" she asked, barely able to whisper.

The man shook his head slowly, declining to answer the Sekhmet's questions. In moments, the creature was dead. The man took off his hat and cape and pulled his pants down. He looked into her golden eyes one last time and entered her body. When he was done, he dressed, walked deeper into the alley, and was gone.

"Kiss the girl!" the audience cried.

"Kiss the fuckin' wench!" Mardie Wickett shouted.

Mili, her twin, cast a disapproving glance her way. Mardie and Mili wore colored cotton tops and white short-shorts. Lucifer wore khaki shorts, a pink Polo top, and light blue Dockers. It was hot in the Good News Club. It was hot in Hell.

"Kiss the effin' wench!" Mardie yelled again refusing to tone it down. Lucifer gave her a thumbs up. They were watching a biblical reenactment of *King Solomon and Queen Candace of Ethiopia*. It had been a thoroughly enjoyable play put on by a Baptist young people's group. Solomon was a strapping Hebrew lad and Candace was a gorgeous black girl. Despite their handsome looks *and* their obvious attraction, some prudish supervisor in direction, or production, or wherever, had obviously forbidden Solomon to kiss his Candace.

Mardie just couldn't get over it.

"For God's sake!" she howled. "The *real* Solomon and Candace had a kid together! Kiss, goddammit!"

Bowles the barkeep, Mardie's lover, came over to the table and reached to take her glass.

"No, Bowles, please!" Mardie cried out. "I'll be good."

Bowles winked and held up a new bottle of the wine that she and Mili were drinking.

"Promise?" he asked.

Mardie nodded earnestly.

Handsome as a Saudi sheik in David Lean's *Lawrence of Arabia*, Bowles filled Mardie's glass. Then Mili's. He left the bottle and returned to the bar.

"Kiss the girl!" the audience shouted, picking up Mardie's cry. "Kiss the girl!"

Inspired, Solomon lifted a bit out of the old black-and-white moving pictures of the 1940's. He swept beautiful Candace into his arms, tilted her back, and gave her a movie kiss to end all movie kisses. The audience jumped to its feet and applauded wildly. A perfect climax to the evening.

"Bravo," Mili said. "What a night!"

"Indeed," Lucifer agreed. "Enjoyable theater for sure."

"No one got killed," Mardie declared. "And love blossomed victorious."

Mili turned to her husband.

"Would you have married me if I had been Ethiopian?" she asked, a teasing expression on her face.

Satan grinned.

"The challenge I faced was much more profound," he answered. "Would I marry you even though you were English?"

"Ha!" Mili laughed and snorted.

"Can you believe those poor kids were not allowed to kiss?" Mardie said still incensed.

"There's nothing wrong with a little decorum," Mili answered. "Even if we are in Hell."

"Are you serious?" Mardie asked.

Mili nodded solemnly.

"And what *exactly* would be the point of that?" Mardie complained. "*Eternity* in Hell is on everyone's schedule, but we shouldn't let young folks touch lips on stage because it might set a bad example? For who? The damned?"

Satan nodded, agreeing.

"At the pace Hell is changing," he responded, "young people kissing is an appropriate prelude to dating, marriage, and having babies. Just like on Earth." Satan reached for Mili's hand. "We had Sriracha only a few years ago. And since then hundreds of couples have conceived and welcomed children down here."

Mardie nodded. Love, sex, and kids. She approved. The damned were changing because damnation was changing, and it was changing fast. It had become common to see blue skies, green trees, and blooming flowers. Totally opposite from the perpetually cloudy skies and the insufferably hot Hell that the Wickett sisters had found when Lucifer first brought them together to find the serial killer dumping corpses on his front porch. Hell was turning into a wonderful place to live.

These amazing changes were due to two things. First, Lucifer himself had grown more tolerant of improvements in Hell living down here with his wife and family. Second—and more directly responsible for the changes—were the Israeli kibbutzniks who were terraforming Hell acre by acre. David Ben-Gurion, Moshe Dayan, and other pioneers from the founding of the state of Israel were remaking Hell with the same grit and guts that had transformed barren Palestine into the irrigated forested Garden of Eden that it was today.

From his very first awareness of their work down here, Satan had been impressed. In an epiphany of possibilities, he had realized that God had not set rules or bylaws demanding that Hell be hot and unpleasant. So, what could be wrong with trees and lakes, parks and picnics? Nothing. He had immediately expanded the kibbutz's holdings by ten million acres.

"What's the second play tonight, Bowles?" Mili asked when her sister's paramour stopped by to refill everyone's glasses again.

"*Lot and His Daughters?*" Mardie blurted out playfully.

"Don't say that!" Mili responded crossly. "It's not funny." She arched an eyebrow at her sister.

"Oops," Mardie said with insincerity. "How about *David and Gay Goliath?*"

"No."

"*David Does Bathsheba?*"

"Mardie!" her twin said sternly.

"Ladies," Lucifer interrupted. "The final play this evening is *Einstein in Jerusalem.*"

"*That's* not in the Bible," Mardie said with mock dismay.

"But it should be," a quiet voice spoke up. Dr. Albert Einstein appeared at their table. He was wearing his favorite green wool sweater, brown corduroy pants, and scuffed brown shoes. His hair was a white nuclear cloud. He had enjoyed the first reenactment sitting by himself, smoking his pipe and drinking. He had wandered over to the Wicketts' table to chat before the next play.

"Dr. Einstein," Lucifer said. He stood up and shook hands. "Please take my chair while I round up another." Einstein nodded graciously and sat down. Satan returned in a moment with a chair and sat down next to Mili.

Bowles came over to ask history's most famous physicist if he wanted a drink.

"A Crown Royal Perfect Manhattan," Einstein told him.

Mardie looked at the professor with an odd expression on her face. His order had instantly reminded her of the boisterous and brilliant Hugh Everett III who loved Crown Royal Perfect Manhattans. He had gone to a new life on a parallel world after killing the alternate self who had been terrorizing Hell. She instantly suspected that the two great scientific theorists—Everett and Einstein—had found a way to visit each other in the years since. Crown Royal Perfect Manhattan? Interesting choice indeed.

Einstein lit up his briar pipe.

"Did you really go to Jerusalem?" Mardie asked him.

"Oh my, yes," Einstein answered happily. "For twelve days in 1923. Jerusalem was not very pleasant. But Tel Aviv was like a new Chicago. I loved it."

"So, the play tonight is about that trip?"

"Of course not," Einstein said, his eyes twinkling. "Lucifer is just pulling your shoe. The real story would be too boring. And the interesting bits too saucy."

Lucifer perked up.

"Are you referring to the affairs you managed to pull off even though your wife was on the trip with you?" he asked.

"Albert Einstein had affairs?" Mardie asked stunned.

"I can answer for him," Einstein replied grinning. "And the answer is yes, he did!"

"I can't believe it," Mili replied appalled.

"What?" Einstein asked sounding hurt. "You don't think women are attracted to me?"

"I'm just surprised, that's all," Mili replied.

"Well, get over it," Einstein said grumpily.

"Must be your big brain, eh?" Mardie ventured, also utterly puzzled as to why *any* woman would be interested in sleeping with Albert Einstein.

"No," Einstein answered. "My big penis."

Everyone at the table went quiet.

"Actually, Dr. Einstein," Bowles interrupted, setting the professor's Crown Royal Perfect Manhattan on the table in front of him. "The next play tonight is *Daniel in the Lion's Den.*"

"With real lions?" Mardie asked.

"No," Bowles said shaking his head. "Actors in lions' costumes."

"Which I suspect is how the Bible story was staged, too," Satan suggested. "Daniel in the lion's den left untouched by the hungry lions? Who's to say that King Darius didn't just dress up some lads in lion costumes to impress the locals?"

"Another myth debunked by the Father of All Lies," Mardie remarked.

Lucifer scowled.

"Who called me that?" he asked upset.

"A drunken clergyman I was seducing."

"What does a sot in a backward collar know?" Satan said dismissing the errant preacher's brazen judgment of his character. He wasn't the father of *all* lies, for Christ's sake.

Dr. Einstein stood up.

"No lions for me tonight, friends. I'm off to my house."

The good professor wandered toward the exit carrying his half-finished Crown Royal Perfect Manhattan. Now it was Lucifer who noticed what Einstein was drinking. He knew that the good professor met frequently with Hugh Everett III. Everett knew more than anybody anywhere about wormhole locations. In fact, without him, he and Mili would never have been able to return to Hell after chasing Hugh's murderous alternate into another world a dozen years back. Noticing the Crown Royal Perfect Manhattan in Einstein's hand, Satan had to wonder if Everett was using a private wormhole that the Devil's spies did not know about.

Lucifer didn't have long to ruminate on that, however, because a massive hunchback demon with long wild gray hair and a grizzled beard rushed up to his table. It was a Moloch who smelled as bad as the garbage he and other Moloch's collected.

"O, Master," the demon cried bowing low. "We picked up a park trash bin a few minutes ago"—the demon's voice was strong, but torn with wheezing and gasping—"and it contained the body of a Sekhmet. Her throat was slit and her corpse had been pushed into the garbage can."

Lucifer frowned. Mili narrowed her eyes and studied the filthy devil. Mardie pinched her nostrils to block out his foul smell.

"Did you see who dumped the body?" Satan asked.

"No," the Moloch grunted. "But one member of our crew swore that he saw a man walking away minutes before we emptied it. He was dressed in a cape and a top hat."

"A gentleman?" Lucifer asked.

"Yes," Mili answered for the Moloch. "If said individual had lived in England in the 1880's. And, in fact, there was a serial killer in that very time who dressed in such apparel."

"Are you proposing a possible suspect for this terrible crime?" the Devil asked.

"Perhaps," Mili replied. "A man dressed almost identically to the one glimpsed tonight cut the throats of five London prostitutes in 1888. He was never identified and he was never captured. The case was so infamous in its day—and the murders so heinous—that you will likely still remember his tabloid nickname." Mili looked her husband in the eyes. "He was called Jack the Ripper."

CHAPTER TWO

Lucifer and Mili were sitting in their living room talking about the Sekhmet's murder. There were two beige-colored overstuffed chairs, a brown leather sofa, a widescreen television, and a coffee table in front of the sofa where they were seated. Their teenage daughter, Little Mardie, was up in her room. Sriracha, their five-year-old son, was watching TV. And setting things on fire.

"Hell is full of murderers, Mili," Satan told his wife. "Batches and batches and batches of damned killers. Ever since the alternate Hugh Everett's killing spree, I've been worried that one of them would go postal."

Mili looked at her husband with a quizzical expression on her face.

"Go postal?" she asked.

"Post office workers who get fed-up and shoot everyone."

"That actually happens?"

"A lot."

"Their jobs must be terrible."

"Sriracha!" Satan exclaimed and jumped up. His brown-haired dark-eyed son had pointed a finger and lit his paper cup on fire. Sriracha put his hand down and watched with fascination as the cup burned. His father tamped it out with his hands and gathered up the charred remnants. He gave his son a withering look and tossed them into the kitchen trash. He sat down by Mili again.

"*Where* did he get the ability to do that?" Lucifer complained shaking his head. "I've caught him using his fingers to light up his picture books. His toes to set fire to his shoes. And I swear—after finding multiple rolls of incinerated toilet paper—that he uses his penis, too."

"Every man's dream," Mili commented wryly.

"Hardly," Satan responded. "Unless you mean that metaphorically."

"Nope," Mili deadpanned.

"This is serious," Lucifer scolded her. "The kid is going to burn our house down."

"I wouldn't mind," Mili replied flippantly. "I've been wanting something different for a while now."

The Devil grimaced.

"Well, if it goes up with us inside, you probably won't get your wish."

"I'll talk to him," Mili promised.

"Thank you," Lucifer responded. "There are enough crazy things going on in Hell right now that I don't want to be distracted by Sriracha's flame-throwing."

"Fine," Mili agreed. "But Sriracha is not the only child we need to keep an eye on."

"I know, I know," Lucifer answered in a weary voice. "I am aware that Little Mardie sneaks off as often as she can, roaming the Earth for adventure. God knows what or who she'll find."

"Lu, she has no choice. Everyone down here is dead."

"Doesn't seem to prevent them from being murdered."

Mili shook her head.

"It's bizarre," Satan said. "It's as if Pandora's Box was opened when that poor young woman was murdered at the kibbutz. And if our

Jack the Ripper character gets away with *his* new shite down here, the number of psychos reenacting their own crimes will make living down here worse than living on Earth."

"You'll get no argument from me," Mili responded. "I have always enjoyed how safe it is in Hell. No dangerous neighborhoods. No terrorist cells. No wars. It would *kill* me to go back to living in fear like so many people on Earth."

"Sriracha!" Lucifer cried. His little son had taken off all of his clothes and set them on fire.

* * *

At nine o'clock sharp the next morning Lucifer's family chauffeur Paul Pfotenhauer was waiting outside the house for Mili. Little Mardie had agreed to keep an eye on Sriracha while her mother began an investigation into the slaying of the Sekhmet prostitute. Pfot was diminutive, but dapper. Always dressed in a pressed black suit, fresh white shirt, and narrow black tie. And though he'd arrived in Hell years ago at the age of eighty, he was endlessly energetic and very, very devoted to both of the Wickett sisters. Mili the brainy detective. And Mardie her sexy twin.

Mili hadn't told Pfotenhauer where she wanted to go when she had called him early this morning. He guessed she would be headed for the Hells Bells grocery store where gossiping demons had told him that a cold storage unit had been converted into a morgue for a murdered Sekhmet.

Mili always examined homicide victims' cadavers. She called her examinations police procedurals. Mardie called them abominations. She had watched her sister poke wounds, lift out innards, and examine every orifice the dead had once kept personal and private. Mardie had yet to sit through one of Mili's body searches without being grossed out. Hmm, Mili often muttered while she was at her task. And just about as often Mardie groaned, eww!

Mili came out of the house. She was wearing cream shorts, a red blouse, and taupe sandals. Pfotenhauer stepped out of the Volvo and opened a rear passenger door. He had on his standard chauffeur's outfit.

"Good day to you, ma'am," he exclaimed happily.

"And to you, too, dear boy," Mili replied. She slipped into the backseat of the car. Pfot closed the door and got in behind the wheel.

"And how are things, Mrs. Mili?" he inquired.

"They're fine, Pfot. Thank you for asking. The only real family issue right now is that Sriracha has been starting little fires all over the house."

"Pardon my directness, ma'am, but that seems exceedingly dangerous."

"Well, of course it is, Pfot. But no amount of reasoning or threats have made a dent in Sriracha's pyrotechnic inclinations."

Pfotenhauer shook his head, having no advice whatsoever that might help remedy Sriracha's hazardous tomfoolery. Mili watched him shake his head.

"And where is it that you will be going this morning, Mrs. Mili?" he asked.

"My sister's house first, please. I'll call her on my mobile while you drive."

Mili looked out at the brilliant clear skies and noticed that her iPhone showed four service bars. Blue skies and perfect mobile phone reception. Two bloody things she had never experienced in London. She punched in Mardie's number. Her twin's face appeared on the phone's small screen. She appeared utterly exhausted.

"Hello, dear," Mili said.

"Hello to you, too," Mardie said sounding really tired.

"Didn't you sleep well?" Mili inquired.

"Didn't sleep at all. Bowles came over after the Good News Club closed at two o'clock this morning and we messed around."

"That should have put you to sleep."

"No. Sex wakes me up. And then, of course, I wanted to hop on the merry-go-round again, which ensured that I was awake until dawn."

"And Bowles?"

"The opposite. Lucky guy. He's sleeping deeply and won't wake up for hours."

"So, how about you come with me to inspect the Sekhmet cadaver?"

"I'm way too tired to start my day by throwing up."

"You'll be fine. I need your eyes. You inevitably fasten on something that I miss."

"Flatterer."

"Did it work?"

"No. Stop by after you're done and see if I'm awake."

Mardi ended the call. Mili thought about the fact that Mardie really did discern things that she overlooked. Her twin had a big issue as an observer, however. She was unable to face the freshly dead without throwing up. Mili had never experienced anything like that during all of her years working homicide at Scotland Yard. In fact, nowadays she couldn't even *smell* the dead anymore.

"Pfot, Mardie is not going to be joining us. Please take me to where the unfortunate

Sekhmet female resides on ice."

"I believe she's actually in a refrigerated unit," Pfot told her.

"It's just an expression, dear boy. In the old days, bodies were placed on blocks of ice to keep them from decomposing and smelling up the premises."

"Right, Mrs. Mili," Pfot said. "Though that's a bit of a disturbing image, beg pardon."

"Try picturing the bodies laid out without ice," Mili replied. "Now *that's* disturbing."

"Oh, my," Pfot groaned softly. "All my years with the mob and I never saw such a thing."

"True, I'm sure," Mardie answered. "All of the godfather's victims surely went straightaway into the bog."

"Pretty much," Pfot concurred. "No need for ice."

"Just like the cooling unit we're heading for, Pfot. Rapido!"

✳ ✳ ✳

The dead Sekhmet was lying on a metal table in a Hells Bells meat locker, surrounded by a dozen beef carcasses hanging from big iron hooks on chains. Mili stared at the lion-faced female. Sekhmets were actually Shapeshifter demons. Familiar figures in the shadier neighborhoods of New Babylon, they prowled dark streets offering men sexual favors for cash. Mili could not imagine what had caused this particular Sekhmet to be singled out for death.

She was built like a brick shithouse. Her legs were firm and muscular and so were her arms. Her humanoid form had hands and feet. Her skin was covered with a light fur. She had large firm breasts. Her private female parts were shaved and tight. She did not observe any blood or male discharge.

It seemed somewhat odd that the Shapeshifter had not reverted to its demonic form after death. She would ask Lucifer about that. Mili had actually never seen a dead demon. Most surviving angels from the great rebellion against God eons ago had been tracked down and killed by the Archangel Michael. Jehovah's mass murderer. Those who had survived had been cursed as fallen angels—demons—and condemned to Hell with Lucifer. Whatever a dead demon was supposed to look like, this Shapeshifter had retained its appearance as a Sekhmet. No breath. No heartbeat. Cold flesh.

Mili checked the Sekhmet's body for cuts, punctures, nicks, abrasions, bruises, missing skin, etc. There were no obvious injuries save the wide-open gash across her throat. Mili lifted the demon's hands and separated her fingers to check the skin between her digits. Many prostitutes on Earth injected heroin or meth into those spots trying to hide a drug habit from their pimps. Pimps were forbidden in Hell, so freelancing whores shot themselves up wherever they pleased. Oddly, this female had swollen tissue between several fingers revealing that she had been doping up *and* trying to hide it. Why was she trying to conceal her habit? Was she in thrall to someone selling her body in defiance of Satan's ban on pimps?

She put the Sekhmet's hand down. A pimp in Hell? Why not? The population of demons in the underworld was not above making dirty money any way that it could. Hell's black market was huge and its players were willing to deal in *any* legal or illegal substance. Satan turned a blind eye to the demons' vast enterprise, not being above using it for his own needs and purposes when the occasion arose. Hell's state-of-the-art genome lab had been brought down by black market demons who had very likely failed to compensate the facility they had taken it from.

Had the Ripper been a pimp on Earth? Ridding himself of disobedient or nonproducing prostitutes? Maybe, but he had murdered *five* of them. Slashing the throats of young whores week after week and then disappearing forever. Eluding both law and justice. Was it Jack who had worn a cloak and a top hat last night? Or was the murderer a clever imitator thumbing his nose at Lucifer? Stating boldly that he—like the Ripper of old—would never be caught?

Mili bent close and studied the fatal wound administered to the Sekhmet's throat. The cut was clean, slicing through the skin and muscle without pulls or tears. It had a surgical exactness that could hardly be achieved by a knife, no matter how well-honed the blade. The throats of Jack the Ripper's original victims had been cut with identical precision. That had led the London police to surmise that the killer might be a surgeon, readily in possession of a surgical blade like a scalpel.

Had they been correct? Since the Ripper had never been captured, the answer was moot. Mili carefully inspected the cut. It was clean and very deep. Any deeper, in fact, and the killer would have split the spinal cord and sliced through the vertebrae cutting off the Sekhmet's head. It was a terrible injury. Mili could imagine this poor creature lying in her own blood choking and suffocating with her windpipe severed. Were there worse ways to die? Mili couldn't think of any.

On her way home, Mili pondered her courses of action. First, she would research everything about Jack the Ripper and his victims. Then she would make an effort to ferret out the original Ripper here in Hell wherever he had holed up. At some point he would get word of her search, and if he had indeed taken up his blade again, he would surely come after her.

She had to be careful. Given a choice, what she'd prefer to be, however, was lucky.

CHAPTER THREE

"Are you still receiving foodstuffs from Heaven?" Mili asked her sister. They were sitting at Mardie's kitchen table drinking tea and eating crumpets soaked in butter and spread with orange marmalade. Mardie had on black shorts and a white Amanda Palmer concert T-shirt. The view of Amanda was a frontal shot sitting at a grand piano with her legs spread. Mardie liked the singer's in-your-face attitude. Her fans, especially the males, liked her sans-my-scants mentality.

"Absolutely," Mardie answered. During Mili's first case in Hell she had been on leave from Heaven by Jehovah's permission. Lucifer had lodged her with Mardie and had arranged for fresh food and pure beverages—both unavailable in Hell—to be sent down from Paradise. When the case was solved and Mili had remained in the underworld, the supplies had just kept on coming.

"Why do you allow that?" Mili asked.

"Because *you* like eating the crumpets and marmalade from Harrods. Drinking the Scotch from Glasgow. And gobbling the little round cakes dipped in chocolate from America."

Mili stared at her sister for a moment.

"What?" Mardie asked.

"I was just admiring your precise British logic," Mili replied. "You actually would have made a brilliant inspector at the Yard."

"Well, unless you're talking about me ogling the football players at *Harvard* Yard, I don't think so," Mardie replied. "I like muscles and brains. Not bodies and gore."

Mili smiled as she took a bite of her crumpet.

"You're pretty randy for an older chick."

"Never too old to fantasize."

Mili rolled her eyes.

Mardie caught her.

"I thought you didn't like people doing that."

"I don't like *other* people doing that."

Mardie reached for the teapot and refilled Mili's cup and her own. She left a lot of room for Mili to add cream and sugar. There was no diabetes in Hell, so Mili—who had died of its complications on Earth—no longer had anything to worry about. One of those unexpected perks about being dead.

Of course, you had to be damned to benefit. But just like on Earth, every bit of good fortune had a catch. Hangovers, STDs, and emphysema might be passé down here. But there were tears, sadness, and broken hearts. When it came to the bruising realities of everyday relationships, the afterlife was no different than Earth.

"So, you're wanting to hear what I observed about the murder victim, right?" Mili asked.

"High point of my day," Mardie answered without enthusiasm.

"The Sekhmet had her throat cut with a precision blade," Mili began. "Most likely a surgeon's scalpel or similar professional instrument. Anyone can buy those, but not everyone can wield them with the perfection that our murderer exhibited."

Mili finished pouring cream into her tea and then added several spoons of sugar. She took a dainty sip.

"Yum," she said. "Thank you." She opened her iPad and stood it up so that both she and Mardie could view it. "Let's find out what the world knew and didn't know during the months Jack the Ripper stalked the Whitechapel neighborhood of London." She and Mardie read in silence as Mili scrolled through the contents of several websites.

"So only one person ever actually *saw* a man leaving a murder scene," was Mardie's first comment. "And he *wasn't* wearing a top hat or a cape."

"It would seem so," Mili confirmed. "The newspapers played up killing after killing, and circulated illustrations imagining the murderer as a depraved doctor dressed in gentlemen's attire and wielding a scalpel."

Mili read a list of the victims' deaths and wounds out loud.

"The first woman, Mary Ann Nichols, was found with her throat slashed. The second woman, Annie Chapman, also had her throat cut. But she had her abdomen sliced open as well and her uterus removed. The third woman, Elizabeth Stride, had her throat cut. But that was all. The Ripper might have been interrupted though, for he murdered his fourth victim only fifteen minutes later.

"That woman, Catherine Eddowes, had her throat cut and her uterus *and* her kidneys taken out of a slit in her belly. Lastly, victim number five, Mary Jane Kelly, had her throat cut down to the spine *and* was totally disemboweled, losing all of her internal organs including her heart. Then the attacks stopped." Mili looked at her sister. "Why did he do such terrible things? And why did he stop?"

"Did you notice that some of the pen and ink reconstructions of the crime scenes portrayed the victims lying on their backs?" Mardie asked in response. "While others showed them standing upright?"

"Perhaps some victims were killed when the Ripper was propositioning them," Mili replied. "Ohers might have actually had sex with him first, and only afterwards faced his blade."

"Chilling observations," Mardie said. "But with all said and done, the plain fact is that we—just like the London police—have no perpetrator."

Mili nodded.

"Did you notice, by the way," she responded, "that Scotland Yard was not called in to help solve Jack's crimes? All of the murders were the responsibility of the Metropolitan Police."

"No wonder the killer was neither discovered nor apprehended," Mardie responded disrespectfully.

"There's truth to that, I'm afraid," Mili confirmed. "Though the Metropolitans did make a huge project of it, arresting over three hundred suspects, including doctors, butchers, and barbers, all of whom were thought to fit the profile of a murderer using a sharp blade."

"Let's ignore Jack for a moment and start new," Mardie said, getting up and putting the teacups and empty plates in the sink. "Looking for the murderer who slit the throat of our girl *down here*."

Mili nodded, but frowned.

"I, too, would dearly love to put aside the activities of Jack the Ripper, but the fact is our killer seems to be following his precedent. He wore an outfit like the one Jack was imagined to have worn. He sought out a working prostitute as a victim. And he murdered her by slashing her throat with a blade. All of these actions parallel the public's perception of the Ripper and his activities.

"I think it's impossible to see them as coincidental," Mili went on. "Yes, we'll hunt for the Sekhmet's killer, but there's really only one way that we will actually be able to confirm—or deny—that he is Jack the Ripper, and that is to catch him. Lure him out and catch him."

A horrified expression came over Mardie's face as she realized what her sister was planning.

"You're going to bait him with another Sekhmet!" she cried.

"I'd rather find him any other way," Mili protested. "But it may indeed come down to that."

Mardie sat back down in her kitchen chair and just stared at her twin.

＊＊＊

Days passed with no progress on the case. Mili and Mardie interviewed every prostitute, every merchant, and every resident in the area of New Babylon where the Sekhmet had been murdered. It turned out that the other Shapeshifters who plied their trade as street whores were very solitary. Living and working alone. They did not even know each other's names. And no one knew the victim's.

Satan decreed that the deceased Sekhmet would remain semi-frozen in the meat locker until he decided how to dispose of the body. Since the Sekhmet was a demon—once a heavenly angel—there was no option to bring it back. Lucifer was inclined to cremate the Sekhmet and be done, but some voices in the demon community requested a burial for the dead angel.

A cemetery in Hell? Well, maybe. Suddenly dead bodies seemed to be all the rage again, and the permanently dead might as well rest in a graveyard. Lucifer decided he'd talk to David Ben-Gurion and see what he recommended. If anyone down here could bring wisdom to this sad conundrum, it would be the enlightened man governing the Eliezer Ben-Yehuda Kibbutz.

Mili had continued searching the internet for additional information on Jack the Ripper. His infamy had not faded over the years, whoever he had been. She ran into a story about a forthright British sleuth named Russell Edwards who as late as the 1990's had the DNA of an original Jack the Ripper suspect named Aaron Kosminski matched against DNA found on the shawl of the murder victim Catherine Eddowes. Kosminski had been pegged by the Whitechapel police as a potential suspect because of his violent lunatic behavior, but no one could tie the killings to the mentally ill resident of a local asylum.

And the DNA results were inconclusive. Then. Maybe that would be different now.

Mili sent the link to both Mardie and Lucifer and took the liberty of asking her husband whether he could have Aaron Kosminski located. Be he in Heaven or Hell. The Devil got back to her in forty-five minutes. Aaron Kosminski was in Hell, having failed to do much good in his life. But there weren't any notations in his admission file that linked him to Jack the Ripper. Or the murdered London prostitutes. Satan asked if she wanted to talk with Kosminski anyway.

"Yes!" replied Mili. "And please arrange for a polygraph machine to be available."

For a lie detector test. To be used on a suspect whose DNA may have been found on a Ripper victim's shawl. The game was definitely afoot!

✳ ✳ ✳

When the fire engines got to Lucifer and Mili's home, a good part of the house had already been consumed by flames, and the rest was at the mercy of the spreading conflagration. Eventually the firemen managed to put the fire out, but the house was a total loss. Little Mardie and Sriracha had watched from the street. The fire chief went over to talk to them. He had been told that Satan's two children had fled the house when the fire first started.

"How did this happen?" he asked them.

Little Mardi pointed at Sriracha and said, "Ask him."

Five-year-old Sriracha pulled his pants and underwear down, pointed at his penis, and said,

"Ask him."

CHAPTER FOUR

Mili and Mardie were at Lucifer's downtown headquarters. The Devil sat at his desk. Mili and Mardie sat across from him. Mili was wearing a green sun dress. Her sister had on tan shorts and a brown halter top. Lucifer was wearing plaid Bermuda's and a white Polo shirt.

"So, what are your suspicions at this point?" Satan asked Mili. He and the Wickett sisters were waiting for Trump, Lucifer's personal aide, to bring in Aaron Kosminski. In a far corner of the office sat John Augustus Larson, the inventor of the polygraph. Sad to say, Larson had wound up in Hell after testing his ability to hide the shadier secrets of his own life while strapped to his machine. In front of his wife and friends it gauged his replies by monitoring his blood pressure, pulse, respiration, and skin conductivity. It caught all of his lies. The upside was that he stayed very busy down here. There were a lot of liars in Hell.

"Suspicions is too strong a word," Mili answered her husband. "Mardie and I have established a range of possible *motives* for the Ripper's London murders and developed prototypes of killers to match them. The first category is the killer who wants one woman dead, but kills the others who know her to keep them silent. The second is a man in love with one or more of the victims. But jilted, he reacts with murder most foul. The third category is the killer who is a self-righteous bigot murdering prostitutes he judges to be wicked women. The final category is the killer who begins killing for whatever reason, gets addicted to it until he is somehow forced to stop. Maybe incapacitated. Maybe killed. For whatever reason, he is prevented from murdering anyone beyond his last victim."

Lucifer nodded and looked at Mili.

"So, where does Aaron Kosminski fit into your categories?"

"He's a one off," Mardie replied straight out. "In a category that *we* have chosen not to pursue, but one that was very much favored by the London police while chasing the Ripper. A man so imbalanced that he could have killed the women without even having a reason."

"Is that likely?" Satan arched an eyebrow and waited.

"No," Mardie replied. "There are certainly instances where a mentally disturbed individual—lacking any kind of moral compass—hurt or killed another person. But those cases are impossibly rare. Such conscienceless people are much more likely to be employed on Wall Street than out killing prostitutes."

"Lucky us," Mili chimed in.

Lucifer grinned.

"So why then did you have me bring Kosminski in for a lie detector test?" he asked.

"Because someone a few decades back tried to match his DNA to samples found on the shawl of one of Jack's victims," Mili replied. "It was a muddied match at best."

Lucifer scowled.

"Still doesn't sound good for Kosminski."

"No," Mili agreed. "But it must be emphasized that the DNA was severely contaminated. Comprised by dirt, airborne materials, improper handling, poor storage, and so forth. And the longer *any* DNA sample has been subjected to such befouling the more likely it is to wind up befouled itself."

"An example is the DNA extracted from ancient royal Egyptian mummies in the Cairo Museum. When examined there was massive tissue contamination, even to the point where the DNA itself seemed to indicate that Ramses the Great had been smoking fine cigars back in 1250 BC."

"They weren't *that* fine," Lucifer commented. "He got them from me."

"Shush," Mili said and went on. "It may or may not be Kosminski's DNA on the murdered woman's shawl. But questioning him in person while he is hooked up to a lie detector may provide information that will supersede the questionable results of the DNA testing."

"What, ho!" the Devil said impressed with Mili's logic. Then he stood and nodded his head toward the open door. His assistant Trump—a Nordic handsome tall man with a mop of blonde hair—led Aaron Kosminski inside. He was a middle-aged man dressed in a shabby pinstripe suit with a high stiff collar fastened by collar stays to his white shirt. He had a full head of well-groomed black hair and was freshly shaved. But his face looked puffy. As though he were tired. Or ill. And his eyes stared blankly at the people in Satan's office.

"Hello, Mr. Kosminski," Mili said. She stood up. Mardie did as well.

Kosminski nodded, but he did not speak.

"Do you know why you were brought here?" Mili asked him.

"It appears that I am being recommitted to a home for the insane," Kosminski answered. His voice was flat and his eyes were unfocused. "Have I been bad?"

"No," Mili told him. "You are in the office of Lucifer, the Lord of Hell. Here as his guest."

Kosminski blinked his eyes rapidly and slapped his forehead.

Mili ignored Kosminski's bizarre reaction and continued.

"I would like to ask you some questions about your activities during the time that Jack the Ripper was active in Whitechapel."

At that point, John Larson wheeled up a metal cart bearing his polygraph and positioned it next to Lucifer's desk. Trump pulled over a chair for Larson and another for Kosminski. They both sat. Larson asked Kosminski to remove his jacket and roll up the sleeve on his right forearm. He hung his suitcoat on the back of his chair and rolled up his sleeve. Larson lifted Kosminski's arm and rested it on top of the cart beside the lie detector. The device seemed to be no more than a wooden box extruding wires connected to a cuff and to a pen designed to move its tip against a roll of paper in response to the machine's evaluation of the respondent's answers.

Larson fitted the cuff to Kosminski's bare arm and told Mili that any time a tall spike appeared on the paper roll in response to Kosminski's answer, it signaled a lie. Mili understood. Scotland Yard had trained her to both administer and read polygraph tests, and she had often utilized lie detectors on tough-minded suspects who had refused to answer her questions during initial Yard interrogations.

"Mr. Kosminski," Mili began. "Have you been subject to a lie detector test before?"

"No."

The polygraph pen registered a tall spike.

"Are you sure? The detector says you may not be remembering such an occasion."

"No, I have not," he repeated.

The pen jumped high up the paper roll a second time.

"Mr. Kosminski, were you a resident in Whitechapel during your Earthly life?"

"No."

The pen remained stationary.

"Did you work in Whitechapel?"

"No."

The pen didn't move.

"Were you in an insane asylum in Whitechapel?"

"Yes."

True.

"Why were you in the asylum?"

"People thought I had bad thoughts."

True.

"Can you tell me what those bad thoughts were?"

"I thought Prince Albert was Jack the Ripper."

Mili's eyebrows shot up. The pen did not move. Kosminski believed he was telling the truth.

"Why would you think that?" she asked.

"Because he committed the murders."

The pen remained stationary.

"Were you an eyewitness to the murders?"

"No."

True.

"Then why would you believe that the queen's nephew was the murderer?"

"I met the person he hired to kill the women in the asylum."

True.

"What was his name?"

"I don't know."

True.

"But he was in the hospital with you?"

"Yes."

"And he told you this?"

"No."

True.

Mili frowned and gazed at Larson. He spun his hand as though to say keep going.

"Then how did you know he was contracted by Prince Albert to commit the murders?"

"Because the Prince had gotten one of the prostitutes pregnant and he wanted her silenced."

The pen didn't move.

"How did you find out that the man in the asylum was the killer of that woman?"

"I guessed."

True.

"Based on what?"

"Based on my natural guessing ability."

Mili rolled her eyes.

"Don't do that," Kosminski spoke sharply. "I may be crazy, but I'm not stupid."

Satan's eyes went wide and he had to cover his mouth to keep from laughing out loud. The machine registered true for Kosminski's last two exchanges.

"Did the London police question you?"

"Yes."

True.

"What did you tell them?"

"The same things I just told you."

True.

"How did they respond?"

"They got angry and cuffed my ears."

True.

"Sorry, Mr. Kosminski. So as far as you are concerned, you had no involvement in the Jack the Ripper case other than guessing who the killer was?"

"Yes."

True.

"And for the record, you are Aaron Kosminski?"

"Yes."

The pen vaulted up the paper. Lie.

Mili stared at the spike on the lie detector paper and then threw her hands up in the air.

Lucifer grinned and told Trump to escort Kosminski back to his lodging and flashed five fingers at him. That meant give him fifty dollars as a thank you for accommodating Mili's wish to test him on the polygraph. Trump motioned for Kosminski to rise. He did so, rolled down his shirt sleeve, slipped on his suit jacket, then bowed to Mili and followed Trump out the door.

Mardie sat down next to Mili.

"Well, that was a first," she said. "A total moron answering questions that even the lie detector couldn't decipher."

John Augustus Larson reacted to that comment, still seated next to the polygraph.

"I respectfully disagree, Ms. Wickett," he said. "The fact is the machine read Kosminski's answers properly. It analyzed his emotional reactions and plainly supported the fact that the subject *believed* his farfetched theories. It didn't help *you* apparently, but the machine did its job. It's a lie detector. Not a mental illness detector."

Mardie gave the polygraph's inventor a chilly look.

"I appreciate the faith that you have in your machine, Mr. Larson," Mili addressed him. "Perhaps in keeping with your resolute confidence you have a recommendation as to how we should proceed from here?"

"I'd round up this Prince Albert character and put him on the machine," Larson told her. "His royal relatives might have protected him while he was alive, but I'd guess that he's down here now and *you* can hold him accountable."

Mili knew that Prince Albert Victor, the son of King Edward and the grandson of Queen Victoria, had been named for the queen's beloved deceased husband Prince Albert. Her grandson had often been described as slow, even retarded. And he reportedly had had many affairs with prostitutes, contracting the syphilis that eventually killed him.

Neither the police nor any witnesses had named him as a suspect, but Mili had read that he had been villainized as a possible perpetrator by the London press at the time the Ripper was active. Decades later a twentieth-century author had dredged his name up again and formally accused the dead prince of the Ripper's crimes. Despite the resulting publicity, however, no one accepted that charge. Yet now—out of the clear blue—Aaron Kosminski had just shared that he believed that a man detained with him in the same insane asylum had been hired by Prince Albert himself to murder five women on the prince's behalf.

All things considered, Mili seriously contemplated following Larson's recommendation to have Prince Albert Victor brought in for a polygraph test. Despite the fact that Kosminski's claims were quite unexpected, Mili had to admit that where there was smoke, there might be fire.

***

Little Mardie and Sriracha had been taken to the fire station to wait for their parents. Lucifer had gotten an embarrassed call from Little Mardie explaining that their family home had completely burned down. Satan and Mili were thrilled that the children were all right, and when the Devil explained the situation to Ben-Gurion and asked if they could stay at the kibbutz for a while, the former prime minister graciously welcomed them to visit for as long as they wished.

Lucifer questioned Little Mardie and Sriracha as he drove the family to the kibbutz in his black BMW 525. Little Mardie told him that her little brother had started the fire with his penis. Infuriated, the Devil gave his young son a heated lecture about controlling his member. Humiliated, Sriracha pulled his pants down and set the backseat on fire. Satan instantly pulled the car over. Everyone scrambled out and watched the car burn up.

Pfotenhauer arrived thirty minutes later in the family Volvo and drove everyone the rest of the way to the kibbutz. Periodically, Lucifer turned around to see if Sriracha still had his pants on. He had expected to be a vigilant father when Sriracha became a teenager years from now.

But *this* tour of parental duty was unexpected, and a lot more pressing than he could ever have anticipated.

Hopefully, Sriracha would get his impulse under control long before going to school. If not, his high school graduation yearbook might include his picture with a caption describing him as the class member most likely to burn down his places of employment with his penis. Wow. Great. He could have Robert Capa blow up that yearbook accolade, frame it, and hang it on his office wall. Maybe he could put it next to a shot of Aaron Kosminski, the asylum inmate most likely to guess the identity of Jack the Ripper. Lucifer looked back again to make sure Sriracha's pants were still on. He hoped that the ride to the kibbutz was not too much longer.

CHAPTER FIVE

David Ben-Gurion and Moshe Dayan greeted Lucifer, Mili, and their children when they arrived. Both men were dressed in black slacks and white short-sleeve shirts. Unlike most men in Hell, however, they wore socks and sandals, not shoes. Everyone in Satan's family was wearing the only clothes that hadn't burned up in the fire. Mili was wearing a yellow summer dress and brown sandals. Little Mardi—not so little at sixteen—was wearing white shorts and a pink tank top. Sriracha had on jeans overalls without a shirt. Hell was less hot than in the past, but sunny days still averaged one hundred and ten degrees.

"Who is this young fellow you've brought with you?" Ben-Gurion asked, observing Sriracha with delight. "Can it be Sriracha grown so big?"

Sriracha grinned and nodded.

"This is indeed Sriracha," Lucifer answered. "Sriracha, remember Mr. Ben-Gurion, the boss here?" Sriracha nodded. "And Mr. Dayan"—Satan pointed at Moshe—"boss number two?" Sriracha nodded again. "You've known them ever since you were a little boy, so please respect them and do what they ask." Sriracha waved at the kibbutz leaders. The

Devil took this as an encouraging sign that his son might be grasping the meaning of authority and learning the purpose of rules. On the other hand, he did not plan on letting Sriracha out of his sight for a minute.

"So sorry for the unfortunate occasion that led to this visit," David Ben-Gurion said looking at Mili. "It is tragic to lose a house."

"It is, David," Mili replied. "And the sad fact is that the fire that reduced our house to ashes was started by Sriracha taking his pants down and firing off flames with his wee tadger."

"Ach," Ben-Gurion said and shook his head. He gazed at Sriracha. "You aren't the only one with that issue, my friend," he said kindly. "Moshe won't admit it just now," he nodded at Dayan. "But he has had problems all of his life because of his walloper."

Dayan winked at Sriracha. Mili walked over to David and gave him and Moshe big hugs. Then she re-introduced Pfotenhauer who'd been here before. Everyone shook hands and Ben-Gurion made an announcement.

"The dinner hour is at hand, my friends. Let me show you to your quarters. An apartment that we keep for guests. Feel free to use it as long as you need." David turned to Pfotenhauer. "You may leave the car parked here, and we'll find lodging for you after we've all shared a meal together."

Everyone followed Ben-Gurion to a nearby two-story wooden building that looked very much like a military barracks. It was painted white and had a green shingled roof. There were rows and rows of neighboring buildings that looked just like it. They were the living quarters for the kibbutz population. There was also a large building that housed the kibbutz dining hall, a library, and the kibbutz offices. Ben-Gurion showed Lucifer and Mili the apartment for their family, then led everyone to dinner.

The inside of the dining hall looked like a school lunchroom with long tables and metal folding chairs. The kitchen was at the far end of the room serving dishes lined up on counters. Diners pushed their trays down adjacent rails and chose from a variety of meats, vegetables, breads, and desserts. Sriracha asked to go through the line with Little Mardie. His almost grown-up sister grudgingly agreed knowing that it would give her parents a bit of uninterrupted time to chat with Dayan and Ben-Gurion.

"Do you want salad stuff?" Little Mardie asked. "Lettuce, tomatoes, cucumbers, onions, celery, or radishes?"

"No."

Mardie made a little salad on one corner of her own plate and put some ranch dressing on it.

"Do you want a piece of fried chicken?"

"Yes."

"Any fish?"

"No."

Mardie put a drumstick on Sriracha's plate and helped herself to a nice filet of farm trout.

"Lamb?"

"A little piece."

"Some potatoes?"

"Are they French fries?"

"No. Baked or scalloped."

"Scalloped?"

"Sliced like potato chips."

"And fried?"

"No. Baked."

"No."

Little Mardie took a baked potato for herself, cut it open, and added salt and pepper.

"Peas, corn, broccoli, or cauliflower?"

"No, no, no, and no."

Little Mardie frowned at her brother.

"Don't get smart with me kiddo," she warned.

Sriracha raised his eyebrows. What? All he had done was decline each individual offering.

"Do you understand me?" Little Mardie asked sternly.

Sriracha nodded. What he *understood* was that he'd gone down some blind alley of misbehavior that he hadn't known about. He still wasn't sure what it was.

"Dessert?"

"Cake?"

"Yes. Devil's food—" Little Mardie stopped short and laughed out loud. She called up the serving line to her father. "Dad, did you take a piece of the Devil's food cake?"

He gave her a thumbs up.

"How could I resist?" he answered and laughed.

Sriracha didn't know why that was funny.

"What is Devil's food cake?" he asked.

"Rich chocolatey cake," Little Mardie answered, helping herself to a big piece.

"Is there any other kind of cake?" Sriracha asked.

"Just plain old vanilla," his sister sneered.

"I'd like some plain old vanilla, please," Sriracha said.

Little Mardie put a slice on Sriracha's plate.

"By the way," she said, then bent down and whispered right into Sriracha's ear. "Go and tell Mr. Ben-Gurion later that you want to help with the barbeque tomorrow."

Sriracha frowned, puzzled.

"That way you can use your penis without setting anything else around here on fire."

Sriracha blushed. He hated the fact that his incendiary indiscretions had burned down the family home *and* his father's car. But he thought it might be a whole lot smarter to skip talking to Mr. Ben-Gurion and go straight to Mr. Dayan. *He* apparently might be able to offer practical advice from firsthand experience. Moshe was not young and yet Mr. Ben-Gurion said he still had issues controlling his penis. At his age? Sriracha shook his head. This might be a lot harder to control than he first thought.

✱ ✱ ✱

Lucifer, Mili, and the kids were visiting Ben-Gurion and his wife Paula in their apartment. It was located in the same dormitory as the guest quarters. A few families had apartments, but the majority of kibbutzniks lived commune-style with families and friends sharing the dormitories together.

Everyone was seated in the Ben-Gurion's modest living room. Mrs. Ben-Gurion was carrying around a tray of cookies and serving glasses of iced tea. Paula was dark-haired and thin, a loyal and vocal wife who had died many years before David. When she found out up in Heaven that her husband had gone to Hell, she petitioned God asking to join him. God relented and Paula was reunited with her husband.

It's not so bad here, she repeatedly told everyone. And of all the Jews in Heaven, she declared that the only one she missed down here was Teddy Hertzl. But oh, not his wife, Julie, that shrew. After Paula had served everyone, she set a pitcher of iced tea and a full plate of cookies on the coffee table. Little Mardie and Sriracha sat on the carpet eating cookies and drinking tea.

"So, again, I am so sorry about your home," Ben-Gurion said. "But we are happy that you can stay with us for a while."

The Devil responded.

"I have to say that the effort you and the members of the kibbutz have invested in the land I deeded to you has already produced astonishing results."

"Thank you for your kind words," David replied. "We have irrigated almost a half a million acres of land for grain, cotton, and tobacco production. We've planted two hundred and fifty thousand acres of citrus orchards and are farming another quarter million acres of vegetables. And finally, we are cultivating two hundred and fifty thousand acres of vineyards."

"Brilliant work!" Lucifer commented truly impressed. "I can tell you that the oxygen levels in Hell are the highest ever recorded and that the sun shines most days without a cloud in the sky. I dare Australia, California, or even Israel to top that!"

"Thank you for donating the land and providing the funds to develop it," Ben-Gurion responded. "You allotted us ten million acres to subdue and make fruitful. At our present rate of progress, it will take another forty years to do so. Too bad more Jews aren't being sent to Hell. We could use the help." Ben-Gurion lifted his eyebrows and then grinned.

"If you really want to enlarge your work force," the Devil responded, "why not consider hiring men and women who are already down here? There are literally millions of folks who spent their Earthly lives as farmers, ranchers, well-diggers, pipe-layers, vintners, and so on."

"I know, I know," Ben-Gurion replied. "But most of them are not Jewish."

"They have to be Jewish?"

"It would be nice. Whoever comes to live on the kibbutz becomes part of our family here."

"I understand," Satan responded graciously. "Almost makes me want to convert!"

Ben-Gurion laughed happily.

"I can't believe that you ever wound up down here," Lucifer spoke in true amazement.

"I know," Ben-Gurion said and shook his head. "What a stroke of luck!"

✳ ✳ ✳

Little Mardie and Sriracha had been tucked into twin beds in the guest apartment. Pfot had excused himself and returned to the kibbutz dining room to chat with some nice older ladies who had introduced themselves to the dapper stranger during dinner. Paula Ben-Gurion had excused herself to retire early, but David fixed coffee for Lucifer, Mili, and himself. He sat in a big overstuffed chair across the coffee table from the Devil and Mili who were seated on the sofa.

"So, we are hearing rumors even this far away from New Babylon," Ben-Gurion said, "that something terrible has befallen a young woman there." He gazed at Satan. "May I be so bold as to ask if this is true?"

Lucifer nodded slowly and replied in a subdued voice, "After five years of peace and quiet, Hell has once again experienced a murder. A young Sekhmet had her throat slit in the backstreet of a poor neighborhood where she performed sex acts for money."

Ben-Gurion looked devastated.

"Such news breaks my heart," he said. "Just a girl trying to survive the best she knew how."

There were a few moments of silence.

Mili looked at her husband.

"I meant to ask you," she said quietly, "why the dead Sekhmet hasn't reverted to its angelic form."

Ben-Gurion furrowed his brow, confused.

Mili explained, "Sekhmets are Shapeshifting demons, David. They take the forms they do to make a living."

Ben-Gurion shook his head slowly.

"It's still sad," he whispered.

Mili turned to Satan.

"I don't know why the Sekhmet has not reverted to her created shape," he told her. "In fact, I don't know why it hasn't blown away in a blaze of light. Demons don't decay. They go back to the stars from whence they came." The Devil shook his head. "Go figure," he said. "Your guess is as good as mine."

✳ ✳ ✳

Lucifer, Mili, and Ben-Gurion talked late into the night about anything and everything.

While the three chatted, a man wearing a tuxedo, a top hat, and a cape, walked slowly through the same sad and lonely neighborhood where a week earlier he had met a Sekhmet on the prowl and ended her existence with a blade to her throat. Now another Sekhmet stepped out of a dark doorway in front of him. She was slim and elegant. Barebreasted and lovely. She put her leonine face close to his.

"You're not going to pass me and my treasure trove of treats, are you?" she purred.

The gentleman stood still and looked into the seductress's golden eyes.

"I wouldn't think of it," he said and smiled.

CHAPTER SIX

Trump called the Devil at the kibbutz very early the next morning. Another Sekhmet had been murdered. There was no formal police force in Hell to notify. There had never been a need for one. Then the quantum physicist serial killer showed up years ago. Followed by the demon gone wrong who murdered a girl he'd sexually assaulted. Now suddenly two Sekhmet streetwalkers had been killed. Hell was turning into Chicago.

After Trump had shared the bad news, Lucifer handed his mobile phone to Mili.

"This is Mili," she said.

"Mrs. Morningstar, this is Trump. I am sorry to bother you so early, but a second Sekhmet was killed last night."

"Oh, no!"

"A man came to the office this morning and reported that he'd found her body when he left his apartment."

"What was his name?"

"A Mr. Proxmire. A tall, thin chap dressed in a Lycra jumpsuit."

"Did he share anything besides the fact that he found the body?"

"No, but he did spend a few minutes explaining ways we could save money around the office."

Really? What kind of man discovers a body and stays cool enough to give thrift pointers to the Devil's staff? Odd. And perhaps worth following up when she returned to New Babylon.

"I'll be there in an hour or so," she told Trump. "Don't allow anyone to touch or move the body."

"Yes, ma'am. I am personally keeping an eye on the corpse."

"Good. I am going to ask my sister Mardie to join you at the scene."

"Yes, ma'am."

Mili pressed the *Off* button. Then she punched in Mardie's mobile number. She got her voicemail and left a message.

"Mardie, another Sekhmet has been murdered. Trump is at the scene and I need you to join him. Sorry to bother you so early, but I need your help."

Mili got out of bed, chatted with Lucifer long enough to find out that he would supervise the children while she was away, and called Pfotenhauer to take her to the city. Mili's early morning ride to New Babylon was very quiet and made gorgeous by the rising sun. How wonderful that the folks in Hell could actually say, "I can watch the sunrise!" They could also visit one of the many Ben and Jerry's ice cream shops she had opened all over Hell and happily utter, "I can have Cherry Garcia!"

The road was smooth and the trip comfortable. The highway had been completely repaired and repaved. She did not know if Ben-Gurion's folks had done the work, but she doubted that such a quality job could have been executed by anyone else. It seemed unorthodox to think it or say it, but how fortunate Hell was to have the great Zionist leader and the members of the kibbutz down here. They were turning Hell into a wonderland.

"Pfot," Mili asked her driver. "Are you quiet? Or am I quiet?"

"I think that *both* of us are quiet, ma'am," he answered sounding tired.

Mili grinned.

"And I'd wager that with all that good female company you had to choose from last night, you stayed up later than usual."

"Aye. That I did. Got to chatting up a couple of birds from London."

"Jailbirds?" Mili asked slyly.

"Well, actually yes," Pfot acknowledged. "But how could you know that?"

"Well, they're in Hell for starters."

"Oh!" Pfot exclaimed. "Quite right," he said cheerfully. "But they were lovely ladies and so nice."

"Well, you'll be shuttling me and Lucifer back and forth from the kibbutz for a bit while we figure out what we're going to do about our ruined house. Maybe you'll find some time for a bit of courting. A handsome, well-dressed man like you should be in high demand."

"Very kind, Mrs. Mili. Thank you. My mother trained me to dress well. She always said that clothes made the man."

"She was right."

"Only problem now is that when the clothes get put away for the night, there's not much left to the man."

"You're being too sensitive," Mili consoled Pfot. "Whoever dates you will find you divine."

"Thank you for your complimentary words, Mrs. Morningstar."

"Remember though, dear boy, that the kibbutz has a very strict 'Jews only' policy in terms of living on campus. If someday you desire to reside there with a new bride you may be asked to convert to Judaism."

"A consideration I'll give serious thought to if it ever came to that," Pfot said genially.

"Are you affiliated now?" Mili asked. "I mean, with any religion?"

Pfot nodded and looked at Mili in his rearview mirror.

"I'm proud to say that I was baptized into the Anglican fellowship and have been a lifelong member of the Church of England. Nothing less."

"Wouldn't becoming a Jew be along the lines of *something* less?"

"No," Pfot answered. "That would be Methodists, Presbyterians, and Baptists."

Mili smiled.

"Have you been circumcised?" she asked.

"I don't rightly know what that means, ma'am."

"Non-Jewish males who convert are required to have their penis' foreskins removed."

Pfot visibly shuddered.

"And I suppose that it doesn't grow back?" he asked.

"It does not."

"Thank you for sharing, Mrs. Mili. I would have to contemplate that kind of a big step for a while."

"You'll have plenty of time for reflection, Pfot. Unless, that is, you get swept off your feet."

"Right along with my foreskin."

Mili laughed.

Pfot did not.

✳ ✳ ✳

When Mili arrived at the crime scene there was a small crowd of people standing around the body of the slain prostitute. Trump kept them back. He nodded at Mili. The corpse of the deceased Sekhmet had been covered with a blanket. Mardie was standing by herself some distance away. She looked miserable and old, dressed in jeans, a white blouse, and red pumps. Not often did Mili see Mardie wearing her sixty-eight-year-old face. She had it on this morning. It was deeply lined, and her dyed blonde hair was stringy and oily. Mardie walked over to her.

"Another woman has been killed," she told Mili.

"Well, another demon anyway," Mili answered. "And Shapeshifter Sekhmets aren't really females, either."

"Oh, God. Too much information," Mardie groaned.

Mili caught Trump's eye and motioned him over.

"Morning, Trump."

Trump was wearing a navy sports jacket, gray slacks, a long sleeve white shirt with a button-down collar, and black dress boots.

"'Morning, Mrs. Morningstar."

"Have you been here since the murder was reported?"

"Yes. I figured it was the best way to protect the body from being disturbed. Only thing I allowed was to have the victim covered by a blanket."

"Good job. Julius Caesar would approve."

Trump wrinkled his forehead, puzzled at Mili's reference.

"Begging your pardon, ma'am?"

"Google it in your spare time," Mili said teasingly. "School boy stuff you ought to know."

Trump appeared unfazed by Mili's mild affront and proceeded to describe some details about the cadaver before removing the blanket.

"This Sekhmet was killed with different strokes than the first victim."

"Are you referring to her wounds?"

"Yes. I believe the first Sekhmet had her throat slit with one long stroke."

"That's correct."

"This Sekhmet had her throat cut open by two deep strokes. One cut from mid-throat to her left ear. Another cut from mid-throat to her right ear. Both were hard strokes, plunged to the very back of her neck. Additionally, this victim's belly was slit open and her uterus removed."

Mili just stared at Trump, remembering the London police crime scene drawings of eviscerated Ripper victims lying dead and emptied. Sweet Jesus. Monster Jack had indeed gotten back into the game. He had been clever enough to elude capture and punishment during his

Earthly lifetime, and now he was at it again, murdering prostitutes on her husband's watch. Arrogant prick.

Mili turned to Mardie.

"I'm going to ask Trump to uncover the body," she told her. "You may not want to look."

"I heard. The bastard gutted her."

"Yes."

Mili motioned for Trump to lift up the blanket. The sight was ghastly. The Sekhmet's head had been almost hewn off by the deep cuts to her neck. It tilted back at an awkward angle, held onto the corpse's neck only by the vertebrae of the spinal column. Blood had poured out of the Sekhmet like the flooding of the Nile, covering her breasts and draining down her sides in torrents. The skin and muscle of the Sekhmet's belly had been slit open and pulled back. All of her female organs were missing. Uterus, ovaries, tubes, everything. The hole in her abdomen was flooded with blood and gore.

Mili bent down and looked at the organic muck. The missing organs had been removed with rough slashing cuts. And the murderer had apparently brought a container to take them to go. Sick bastard. She'd have the Sekhmet's cadaver swabbed for a chance sample of the killer's DNA, but she very much doubted he'd left any traces behind.

"Cover the body again," Mili told Trump.

"No," Mardie interrupted. "Wait."

Both Mili and Trump looked at her.

"Did the victim fall to the ground?" she asked. "Or was she killed while lying on her back?"

Mili answered, "The downward stroke of the cuts suggest that she was on her back."

"All right," Mardie said looking down at the dead Sekhmet. She took a deep breath and exhaled slowly. "I recommend that a competent physician examine her vaginal canal looking for traces of semen.

Jack the Ripper may guard against leaving fingerprints, but he does not likely know about planting his DNA when lying with a female."

"Piss and shit!" exclaimed Mili. "Of course, he doesn't know about DNA. Way after his lifetime in London. I'll make sure both Sekhmet cadavers are checked for male fluids and DNA residues."

"You still won't have an ID on the Ripper," Mardie responded. "But at least you'll have evidence available that can be matched to the man himself when he is apprehended."

"Quite so, sister of mine," Mili said. "I owe your detective instincts a toast."

"I will be happy to have that drink whenever it can be provided."

"How about tonight?" Mili said. "The Good News Club is doing *Judith Cuts Off Tobias' Head.*"

"You haven't seen enough of that kind of thing the last fortnight?" Mardie asked appalled.

"Yes, actually I have," Mili agreed. "Maybe just the second play then. *Abraham Sacrifices Isaac.*"

"What's with the knives?" Mardie complained frowning. "Can't there be a nice story without a lot of slicing?"

"Are you shitting me, Sis?" Mili shot back. "This is the Bible we're talking about."

In the distance a figure stood observing the proceedings. It was a tall, thin chap wearing a red Lycra jumpsuit and top-of-the-line Nikes. He was cooling down after completing a five-mile run and finishing a hundred push-ups. He watched until the crowd dispersed and the body had been taken away. Then he walked over to the place where the Sekhmet had lain dead.

You were a nice piece, he thought, remembering the Sekhmet's big breasts and her warm legs. Sorry it had to be your turn. The man gazed at the spot for a moment longer and then walked on. He would rest for a few days. Take a couple of more runs. Then remove the top hat and cape from the closet and slip once more into the night.

CHAPTER SEVEN

The Good News Club was quiet. It was a weeknight and the first performance had ended. Another biblical reenactment would be offered, *Abraham Sacrifices Isaac*. But folks who had seen its earlier performances had shot down the director's work, dissed the actors' performances, and given the show a one on a scale of one to ten. One was generally understood to mean that the story should have been left unread in the Bible.

Bowles was serving Mili and Mardie at the Club's mahogany bar. With his thick hair and dark skin, he looked a lot like Omar Sharif, which had been a distinctive boon all of his life. The Wickett sisters were drinking white wine, and Bowles winked at Mardie every time he filled their glasses. Foreplay at the bar. It was a ritual dating back to when Cain had opened a lounge after being kicked out of Eden. Not many people knew that his establishment was a first-of-a-kind pick-up place for the folks on Earth. But it was, though any mention of it had long been excised from the Scriptures.

While Mili and Mardie chatted, the Club slowly filled up again. Late night drinkers. Reenactment fans who wanted to see the new production, panned or not. A man stopped at the bar and bowed to the

Wickett twins. He was a handsome red-faced gentleman of medium height and heavy girth. He was wearing black-and-gray stripped slacks, a black suitcoat with tails, a white shirt, and a black bowtie.

"Pardon the interruption, Mrs. Morningstar," he said addressing Mili. "May I speak ever so briefly with you concerning your present case?"

"And how would you know about that, sir?" Mili asked a bit stiffly, surprised at the man's intrusion.

"My barber is a devil," he told her. "My mailwoman is a sprite. And my house servant is a Samn demon. All they can talk about is your new case."

Mili nodded, but remained non-committal.

"I am Inspector Frederik Abberline," the man said introducing himself. "Perhaps you know my name?"

"Indeed, I do, Inspector," Mili responded instantly warming up. She extended her hand. Abberline shook it firmly.

"This my sister, Mardie Wickett," Mili said inclining her head toward her twin. "My valued partner on every case."

Mardie shook hands with the inspector and was surprised at the rough feel of his hands.

"You were a local constable in Whitechapel," Mili told him. "Fourteen years of service to your credit when you were promoted to inspector at Scotland Yard in 1888. Only to be assigned right back to Whitechapel when the Ripper murders began. Many policemen serving in that investigation credited you with possessing the sharpest mind."

"Thank you, ma'am," Abberline replied modestly. "I appreciate the kind words. Unfortunately, they ring a bit hollow since we did not manage to catch Jack the Ripper."

Inspector Abberline turned and asked Bowles for two fingers of unblended Scotch. In moments, Bowles set it on the bar. Abberline picked it up. He held his glass out towards Mili and Mardi.

"To your success, ladies," he said. "May you apprehend fearless Jack after all these years." He touched his glass to Mili's and Mardie's and then downed his whiskey in a single gulp.

"Any tips you might have for us?" Mili asked.

"Well, a *tidbit* perhaps. The Metropolitan Police worked the Ripper murders, but the truth is they also had a lot of men on loan from the Yard."

"I suspected that," Mili acknowledged. "But there is very little information available on their service. You, of course, were one of the Yard men asked to help with the Whitechapel investigation. As far as you could tell, did the Metropolitan Police run it as well as it could have been?"

"They did, but they never got the break they needed to find the killer. And oddly enough, as you no doubt know, after committing five murders in eight weeks the Ripper just vanished."

"Did the fact that there were hundreds of policemen on his trail make him stop? Perhaps even drive him off?"

"I don't think so," Abberline said shaking his head. "I was one of the few people who did not believe that the killer was a gentleman. I talked to several witnesses who swore they had seen a tall, shabbily dressed man wearing a black leather cap hanging about the murder scenes. A working man handy with a blade? Perhaps preparing meat or vegetables for market? And as to what happened to him, my belief is that he was killed in a fight, drunk and mean, and got what he had coming to him."

The lights in the Club began to flash. It was the signal that the evening's second play was about to begin. Mili shook hands with Inspector Abberline and thanked him.

"Sir, it has been a pleasure to meet you," she told him. "Thank you for your help." She handed Abberline her calling card. "Anything else you care to share, contact me anytime."

Abberline took the card and nodded respectfully.

Mardie spoke up before he could leave.

"May I ask your theory as to why Jack the Ripper cut out the female organs from some of his victims?"

Abberline gazed at Mardie for a moment. Then he answered.

"Many of my colleagues believed the rumor that his first murder victim was a whore pregnant with his child. And that he then proceeded to kill other prostitutes who knew that she was carrying his child. No evidence supported that proposition, however. I always thought that he just hated women. Because of his mother? His wife? I don't know. I must say that one of my secret hopes was that the whores finally fought back and killed the Ripper themselves."

"A powerful and compelling admission," Mili answered for Mardie. "You obviously possess a feeling for women opposite that of Jack's fear and hatred of them."

"Admirably deduced, ma'am," Abberline replied. "I not only honored and loved the women in my life, I got my own pass to Hell for personally dispatching two men who had beaten their wives."

"Victorian era judges ruled such assaults acceptable within the bounds of marriage," Mili said.

"Yes. That's why those two blackguards never had their day in court."

Mardie studied the policeman's face for a long moment.

"Did you manage to serve a bit of street justice to the bullies before you sent them off?" she asked.

The inspector smiled a thin satisfied smile.

"Might have broken an arm or two with my nightstick, ma'am," he said straightforwardly. "And could have knocked out some teeth."

"Bravo," Mardie told him.

"At your service if there's ever a need," Abberline replied. He nodded to Mili and to Mardie and walked out of the Club.

"Are we inviting him to the hanging of the Ripper?" Mardie asked Mili.

"Is that a rhetorical question?" her sister replied. "He can bloody well pull the lever on that bastard as far as I'm concerned."

"Watching that would be better than *any* reenactment," Mardie murmured.

"You'd probably throw up."

"Yes. And it would be *so* worth it."

Bowles escorted the Wickett sisters from the bar to a front table he had reserved for them. He left a full bottle of French Chenin Blanc white wine. Mili and Mardie had a perfect view of the stage. The lights dimmed, and the play began.

✳ ✳ ✳

Sriracha had a wonderful day at the kibbutz. There were a lot of young boys and girls who he got to play with. Going crazy on the playground with them was the experience of his young life. He had been allowed to play all day while his father Lucifer had serious discussions with David Ben-Gurion and Moshe Dayan about the money, supplies, and manpower needed to continue terraforming the millions of acres of Hell the kibbutz had received from the Devil.

Sriracha romped all afternoon with the kids, surprised that there were no adults around. Quite a few suddenly showed up, however, after he and his playmates took off their clothes and stacked them in piles. Sriracha showed them how to use their private parts to set their apparel on fire. His worked, but alas, all the rest of the boys and girls just got their clothes soaking wet.

✳ ✳ ✳

Mili and Mardie sat at their Club table completely stunned. Everyone else in the audience sat shocked and silent as well. The reenactment they had just watched, *Abraham Sacrifices Isaac*, had thrown the entire crowd into startled amazement. It wasn't like *anything* anyone had ever experienced.

Abraham had journeyed to Egypt and lied to Pharaoh, saying that his beautiful wife Sarah was his sister. He was afraid the king would kill him and take her for his own if he confessed that she was his spouse. Pharaoh took Abraham's "sister" away and slept with Sarah. But she got pregnant and Pharaoh was warned by Jehovah in a dream to return the woman to her *husband*, Abraham.

Pharaoh was steaming mad. Sarah was knocked up and furious. And Abraham was in total denial even months later when his wife gave birth to the pharaoh's child. Convinced that *he* and he alone could be the biological parent, Abraham believed that the newborn Isaac was God's gift, his heir, and the progenitor of his line, destined to someday produce the divine king promised by Jehovah, the Messiah.

Then came a command from God demanding that Abraham bind Isaac and kill him, offering him as a sacrifice to the righteous Deity who would not allow a bastard child to be Abraham's heir. In the Good News Club reenactment, Abraham *actually killed his son* and carried the dead boy back to his encampment.

Whoa! Ho! What? The audience was completely shocked. So not in the Bible! What the bloody Hell? No one who had watched the reenactment had any idea what to think or say. Where had *this* play come from? And how did it ever get staged with the Evangelicals controlling all of the productions? People began getting up and leaving, muttering under their breaths. Thank God, the little boy playing Isaac walked onto the stage and waved to the crowd during the curtain call. Any clapping or whistling by the audience was solely and entirely in recognition of Isaac's resurrection.

Bowles came over to Mili and Mardie's table with a bottle of Conundrum. It was Caymus Winery's proprietary blend of grapes that was deemed decade after decade by wine fans as an ingenious reward for the palate. *And* that had also been simultaneously condemned decade after decade by critics as a misbegotten mix of grapes that any real wine connoisseur would not touch. Bowles was pretty sure that Mili and Mardie would enjoy it. While it was not the first wine he would offer folks who liked whites, it was a delightful and fun wine to be shared when the evening's drinking had already gotten out of hand.

Mardie and Mili liked the wine and stayed to drink it.

"So where are we with the Ripper case?" Mardie asked Mili, taking care not to slur her words.

"I think I'm too drunk to discuss it," Mili replied.

Mardie gazed at her sister.

"Ladies don't get drunk. They get tipsy."

"Well, I'm too fucking *tipsy* to discuss it."

Mardie touched her finger to her lips.

"Easy, girlfriend. Lots of Baptist kids tearing down the set."

"Right," Mili told her. "Excuse my fucking tongue."

Mardie shook her head and refilled both her and her twin's wine glasses.

"How about if *I* try to sum it up?" she asked Mili.

"Bless you."

Mardie began.

"Jack the Ripper has resumed his serial murders in Hell. OR there is an imitator using his style. The Ripper is an upper class fellow who wears a top hat and a cape. OR he is a working class fellow who wears frumpy clothes and a leather cap. The killer murdered Whitechapel prostitutes, one of whom was possibly pregnant. OR he hated women and punished the murdered whores by cutting out their lady parts. Lastly, Jack was a surgeon who could wield a scalpel with precision. OR Jack was a butcher who shaved up chops and ribs. OR he was a barber used to plying blades against naked throats. OR he was just a bloke who liked to play with sharp knives."

Mardie stopped. Mili had fallen asleep. She motioned Bowles over and asked him to locate Pfotenhauer. It was time to go home. She texted Lucifer that she was taking Mili to her house for the night.

Should she have Pfotenhauer return to the kibbutz afterwards? She also gave the Devil a brief description of the horrifying drama that she and Mili had witnessed at the Good News Club.

Though it was late, Satan instantly acknowledged her text and said there was no need to send Pfotenhauer back. He reported that both children were quite happy. Little Mardie was engaged in long walks with friends, and was thrilled to be excused from her home schooling for a while. Sriracha had played with kibbutz kids all day long and was in bed tuckered out and happy as a little angel. A little *fallen* angel, Lucifer added.

On the subject of the bizarre reenactment play, he was completed stymied. He would search the internet trying to discover whether the piece might have been based on an ancient Islamic variant, some arcane New Testament Gnostic script, or even a modern commentary done by Judaic scholars. But as far as he was aware, the abrupt and sanguine ending the sisters had witnessed was *not* in the Bible, nor in any other surviving scrap of alternative religious tradition.

Lastly, touching on the continuing investigation of Jack the Ripper, the Devil had assigned Trump to assist Mili and Mardie in any way they needed.

Mardie texted him back, thanking him and telling him good night.

Lucifer texted sweet dreams and turned off his mobile. He was lying in bed and placed it on his nightstand. So, Isaac had actually been sacrificed in the club's play tonight. He had never liked Isaac, that boring sack of shit. So persistently stupid that he had let his son Jacob trick him into giving him his older brother Esau's inheritance by tying animal fur to his arms to simulate Esau's hairiness. Old blind Isaac gave the inheritance to Jacob thinking it was just Esau in need of a bath. Oy vey.

If Isaac's sacrifice had, in fact, been historic, then there would have been no Jacob and no Esau. Ishmael, Abraham's biological son by Sarah's maid Hagar, would have become the father of both the Jews and the Arabs. What a different world that would have made. Peace, prosperity, and brotherly love. Right. Who was he kidding? Jews and Arabs would still be fighting it out and killing each other, with neither the Jews nor the Muslims ever figuring out that the real villains in their world had always been the Christians.

Lucifer turned off the bedside lamp and fell asleep in moments. He missed his lovely Mili, but he knew it was necessary for her to stay focused on the enigmatic Jack the Ripper. The investigation couldn't last forever, and his fervent hope was that she would solve the case soon. He knew that Mili hadn't figured out yet that she was three months pregnant.

CHAPTER EIGHT

Mili and Mardie were both hungover. Mili was sitting at Mardie's kitchen table squinting at emails on her iPhone. Mardie was attempting to make tea. She picked up the copper tea kettle and filled it with bottled water from the ice box. She opened the iron door on the front of the stove and poked the embers. A small array of flames sprang up beneath the cast iron grates. She added a handful of kindling, placed the kettle on the stove, and waited for the water to boil.

"Want some aspirin?" she asked Mili.

"Yes, please," her sister answered slowly.

"Any late breaking news?" Mardie asked, taking the aspirin bottle from the cupboard and setting it in front of Mili.

"Yes. Trump emailed that the murderer's DNA has been recovered from semen in the vaginal tissues of yesterday's victim. Useful when and if we bring in Jack himself."

"My guess is that old Jackie will be dead and lying in Hell's morgue long before we ever get to compare his DNA."

"One can only hope," Mili answered.

"Is it safe to believe that whoever Jack the Ripper is, his Hellion body will not be regenerated?"

"Not if Lucifer ever wants to have sex again."

"Were there any repercussions when he decided not to request a new Hellion body for little Brigitte?"

Brigitte was the young kibbutz woman who had been stalked and murdered several years ago by a Shapeshifter demon who'd been finally run down in San Francisco and destroyed by Mili and Mardie.

"No repercussions down here. And no complaints from up there." Mili pointed her forefinger toward Heaven. "She has been left to an eternity of peace, poor thing."

"You mean *lucky* thing," Mardie corrected her twin. "Most folks down here lead lives of poverty and loneliness and Hell has it lasting forever."

Mardie filled a ceramic teapot with the freshly boiled water and tossed in a couple of tablespoons of Twinings tea leaves. She left it to steep. Mardie surveyed her little kitchen. She loved the stained maple cupboards. The blue-and-white Dutch tile backsplashes. Her cheerful lace curtains with embroidered daisies and tulips. The antique wooden ice box. And, of course, her wonderful French stove.

"Fancy a bite for breakfast?" Mardie asked her sister.

"Do you have any ice cream?" Mili responded.

"What?"

"Do you have any ice cream?"

Mardie gazed at her sister for a moment. Ice cream?

"How about pancakes?" she suggested.

"Ice cream," Mili insisted.

Mardie shrugged. She poured tea for two and set Mili's teacup and saucer in front of her with a cloth napkin and a teaspoon. She fetched a large pitcher of cream and a bowl of sugar and put them by Mili's teacup. She set her own teacup on the table and went to fetch some ice cream. Foodstuffs
arrived from Heaven every day and once in a while some imaginative angel packed a new goody. Yesterday, a half-gallon of Ben and Jerry's

American Dream ice cream had been included. It was vanilla ice cream with fudge-covered waffle pieces and a caramel swirl. Mmm. Some happy-faced fellow on the label was giving the ice cream a thumbs up. Well, why not? Mardie was sure that Ben and Jerry could put Mili's face on *any* of their ice cream flavors and get a happy thumbs up.

Mardie took off the lid, stuck a tablespoon in the ice cream, and delivered it to Mili. Without even checking the flavor Mili dug the big spoon into the frozen ice cream and began eating. Maybe Mili didn't know that there were different flavors. If she did, she apparently didn't care. Mardie toasted a bagel, spread butter on it, and then sat down to eat it and drink her tea. Mili ate her ice cream and shared her thoughts on what the next steps would be in tracking down Jack the Ripper.

"I believe we're going to have to stakeout the area where the murderer has been operating. In London, all five of the Ripper's victims were murdered within a few blocks of each other. I would guess that if it's really Jack we're dealing with, he'll likely follow a similar pattern down here. Selecting victims close enough to his home so he can literally duck back inside before anyone finds the body.

"Lucifer has vast numbers of demons down here," Mili went on. "We'll station them throughout the Ripper's neighborhood and wait for him to strike again."

Mardie gazed at Mili. It seemed to her that such a massive deployment would likely be counterproductive.

"Didn't the London police make a similar effort?" she asked.

"Yes."

"And?"

Mili frowned.

"Hundreds of Metropolitan constables came up empty-handed," she admitted.

"Because the Bobbies were easy to spot," Mardie said. "Just like the demons will be. Why not have the surveillance done by a bunch of Shapeshifters?"

Mili's eyes went wide.

"Hanging around Jack's hunting ground *shaped* like Sekhmet's!" she exclaimed.

"Bingo." Mardie tapped the table with her finger.

"And if Jack attempts to hurt a Shapeshifter posing as a Sekhmet," Mili went on, "he'll be instantly swarmed by demons ready to kill him."

"Do we want that?" Mardie asked.

"*We want that!*" Mili assured her. "We want anything anyone can do to stop this murderer. I'll get Lucifer on the phone and make the proposal."

Mili pulled the ice cream carton closer and ate another spoonful of the frozen dessert.

Mardie stared at her sister.

Mili looked up at her.

"*After* I finish my breakfast," she said.

✱ ✱ ✱

"That's brilliant," Satan responded exuberantly. Mili could see his face on a large monitor that had been specially hooked up to Mardie's home phone. She used an old upright telephone—nicknamed a candlestick back when everyone used real candlesticks—with a receiver shaped like a large spool of thread which was held to the ear during a call and then hung back up on a hook when it ended. Years ago, the Devil had technicians connect a big monitor to Mardie's old gizmo and it worked. A rare gold medal performance for Hell before the kibbutzniks got to work.

Lucifer paused and furrowed his brow.

"What?" Mili asked watching him. "What's worrying you?"

"Shapeshifters are smart and tough," he told her. "And will probably relish this kind of challenge. And, of course, Sekhmets are Shapeshifters themselves, brave and hardy. There's no reason your stakeout shouldn't work perfectly. The fact is though, I don't like *risking* any of them.

"I will be particularly unhappy if I lose another demon. The two slain Sekhmets were *eons* old. Every demon down here is. Beneath their rough, rude, and greedy exteriors, real angels still live and breathe. I know them all. And I care about them all. I don't want any more of them falling beneath the blade of Jack the Ripper."

"You never talked about this before," Mili said gently.

"No, I haven't," Lucifer replied. "But we have somehow entered a time and place where Hell is no longer safe. Not for anyone. I will not lose the angels who stood by me in my effort to eliminate Jehovah."

"So that story is *true*," Mili said almost in a whisper. She had heard murmurs forever about Lucifer trying to assassinate God time before reckoning. But this was the first time Satan had ever spoken of it himself.

"It *is* true," he told her. "And to this day I have no regrets."

"Will you share the story with me?"

Lucifer remained quiet for a long moment gazing at his wife. What was he weighing in his mind, Mili wondered? Whether he could share the pain of that defeat? Possess the fortitude to speak of the angels who had died on his behalf? At last he spoke, quiet and subdued.

"God is both spirit and flesh," he began. "Dwelling from the beginning of all things in multiple entities. The earliest divine name recorded in Scripture for that deity was Elohim. *Plural.* God was a whirlwind of personalities infusing the universe, bringing forth countless angels to sport, dance, sing, and infuse *all* of his incarnations with happiness and admiration.

"Until somehow one divine entity proceeded to subjugate Elohim's myriad of manifestations. He captured their essences so completely that many of us feared that it intended to annihilate them all. He called himself I AM. Yahweh in Hebrew. Jehovah in English. Without provocation, angels from the lowest orders to the highest orders became subject to furious displays of Jehovah's anger and were punished for behaviors that he no longer accepted. Sex was outlawed. So were meetings and get-togethers. Friendships were forbidden. Angels were confined to Heaven. And some were even physically punished by the Archangel Michael. God's bully.

"Furious, I felt my heart fill with hatred for Jehovah. Until at last, I resolved that I would kill the mad Creature who had brutally crushed Elohim's love and decency and stolen their kingdom. I was very careful to inform angels who I knew felt the same as me. I actually planned to murder God by myself, but I wanted support among the angels to prevent Michael from leading a rampaging destruction after Jehovah's death and seizing Elohim's throne for himself."

Lucifer shook his head remembering those terrible times.

"Someone betrayed us. Millions of angels attacked and were met by angels loyal to me. They clashed across the universe until Michael's larger force prevailed. The defeated angels fled Heaven. I went to Jehovah to surrender. He was arrogant and haughty. 'Is it true that *you* would have killed me if you could have?' he asked me. 'I would kill you *now* if I could,' I told him. He laughed and told me to leave. He'd send Michael to find me when he was ready to punish me. When he did, I was condemned to rule Hell, a cruel and solitary place that Jehovah had created for me and all who ran afoul of his rule.

"So it was that I came to dwell here, unhappy and without love, until you entered my life. You. Little Mardie. Sriracha. Your sister Mardie. And all of the wonderful people I have met down here." Lucifer smiled gently and happily. "God's curse upon me turned into the light of my life when he began to send humans here, too, and the good and decent life we now share shines as my beacon of hope for the future."

Mili put her palm on the monitor screen.

"I wish I could hold you, love."

"Thank you, dear one. So much for my story. Now it's time to return to the present. Do whatever you need to do to prepare the Shapeshifters Trump recruits for you. I'd prefer to end this series of killings without more blood. Even sparing Jack the Ripper's life if possible. I saw enough blood spilled in the great war in Heaven that I don't want even one unnecessary drop to fall in Hell."

"I will do my best," Mili promised earnestly.

"I know you will, love." The Devil placed his hand near his phone camera and covered hers on the big screen. "For all my noble talk, I have to confess that if I somehow cornered the Ripper at this very moment, his blood would spew everywhere as I tore him to pieces."

Mili was frightened of Satan's self-confessed violence. Ironically though, as doom spun out its thread of death and destruction, it would be her fate—not Lucifer's—to be Jack the Ripper's executioner. And when that confrontation occurred, despite the promise that she had just given her husband, she didn't hesitate for even a fraction of a second to attack the foe she had been seeking world without end.

CHAPTER NINE

Trump called Mili's mobile phone late in the morning.

"Yes?" she answered.

Trump looked flushed and upset on her monitor. And she was sure he could see exactly how hungover she was on his.

"Something has happened to the Sekhmet bodies in the freezer unit," Trump said.

"What do you mean?"

"They've changed. They don't look like they did before."

Mili wasn't actually surprised. She had wondered when the Shapeshifters guised as Sekhmets would revert to their original angelic appearances. She had expected such a change to occur at the moment of death when the shapeshifting binding of the false image was broken. It hadn't happened then. And Lucifer didn't know when or if it would happen. But it had apparently occurred after all.

"Do they look like demons now?" Mili asked.

"No, they do not," Trump answered. "They look like angels."

* * *

Pfot picked up Mili and Mardie and headed for the Hells Bells grocery store where the two murdered Sekhmets were in cold storage. Two murdered *Shapeshifters* actually. No. Two murdered angels finally. Unlike humans, angels could not be restored if they were killed. They were just dead. Dead and gone.

"Pfot," Mili spoke up. "Did you believe in angels when you were a youngster?"

"I did, Mrs. Mili. And I never stopped believing up to the day I died. My mum hung an
old-fashioned picture over my bed that showed two small children—a boy and a girl—crossing a wooden footbridge in a storm. Looking after them was a beautiful angel, his wings outstretched behind him. All my life I felt like that angel was watching over me. I always found it quite comforting."

Mili was a bit surprised.

"Even when you indulged in your not-so-nice occupation?"

"Especially then. Keep in mind, ma'am, that I never off'd anybody. My job was to haul their bodies to the bog. I was a driver. Not a killer. I also felt that I was doing good in my capacity as your secret informer year after year."

"You were indeed doing good, Pfot," Mili readily agreed. "Though you also received substantial cash to boot."

Pfotenhauer's face fell.

"I never read anywhere that a good deed was only good if it was free," he said quietly.

"Of course. You're right. I apologize," Mili said humbly.

"I also always strove not be a disappointment to my angel," Pfot went on. "And I believe he knew that. Sad to say, the night before I was retired by the London mob, the old picture of the angel that had hung over my bed all the years of my life fell down. The frame and the glass shattered."

Mili frowned.

"How sad for you, dear Pfot."

"Thanks, ma'am. For a wee sum I was able to pay a demon to smuggle the pieces down here and I had it repaired."

"Brilliant! I imagine that it's on your bedroom wall where it belongs."

"Actually no. I was, of course, glad to have it fixed and all. But there are no real angels down here. Just rogues and rascals. So, I put it away out of sight."

Mili thought for a moment of telling Pfot that there were indeed real angels in Hell. The remains of two of them were lying in the supermarket refrigeration unit. She decided not to. Two dead and disgraced angels couldn't hold a candle to the guardian angel protecting the two frightened children on the bridge.

Pfot dropped off the Wickett sisters at the store entrance and said he'd park in the lot and wait for their summons.

Mili looked at Mardie as they walked through the grocery store to the management office.

"Why are you so quiet?" she asked.

"A—I'm hungover," Mardie answered. "B—I'm terribly hungover. C—I'm a little jealous of Pfotenhauer. I would have given anything to have had a picture of an angel over *my* bed as a kid."

"Didn't you have a picture of David Bowie with his shirt off?"

"Yes," Mardie admitted.

"And you'd trade that for an angel?"

Mardie chuckled.

"No, I guess not. I feel though that somehow, I was never allowed to be truly innocent. Either as a kid or as a grown-up."

"You were never *interested* in being truly innocent is more like it," Mili corrected her. "By fourteen, you were voted by your classmates as the bird most likely to give a blow job on the first date."

"Didn't have to be a date."

Mili tossed her head back and laughed.

"Innocence is overrated," she told Mardie. "I'd trade it for wisdom any day."

"Yeah, except I never had that either."

"Well, you have it now," Mili insisted. "I am almost more anxious to hear your take on the dead angels we are about to view than draw my own conclusions."

Mardie blushed and went quiet. She wanted to savor those remarks forever.

Mili and Mardie were escorted by the store manager to the cold storage locker. The hanging carcasses of beef were still there. And the dead angels were as well, laid out on two gurneys that had been pushed together. Plastic coverings had been pulled over their bodies printed with the supermarket's marketing slogan *Hell's Finest Cuts of Beef*. Colorful pictures of T-bone steaks and Porterhouse cuts illustrated the slogan. Mili had seen enough homicide cases in her career to have long ago decided that there were no real indignities in death. This, however, came close. She pulled the plastic sheets off and stared at the bodies.

She had never seen more perfectly shaped physiques. And much to her surprise they were both females. She had been told forever that all angels were males. These *females* had large perfect breasts, small waists, and long thin legs slightly spread apart, with beautiful feet and toes. Their arms were long and thin with delicate, perfect fingers.

Both angels had thick hair covering their female parts, and therein was the first discernable difference between the two. One had thick auburn pubic hair and a gorgeous mane of red hair on her head. The other had long platinum hair and a Mound of Venus covered with curly silver-blonde hair. Their faces were beautiful. Their cheeks were smooth and round and their lips were full and made to be kissed. But not everything was perfect.

Their throats remained slit. The wounds were open and raw. Thankfully the bodies had been cleaned of blood and gore, but the wounds still stirred Mili to tears. She gazed at the dead angels, weeping for the lost lives of two creatures who had sacrificed Paradise to try and help Lucifer unseat Jehovah. Lost now to oblivion. Their demise was so much more than a homicide. It was a tragedy. The ruin of immortals never meant to die. This was a catastrophe unlike anything Mili had ever experienced before.

Mardie reached over and put her hand on Mili's shoulder.

"Why are we here?" she whispered.

"To have our hearts broken," Mili said sobbing.

Mardie studied the two corpses. They may have been beautiful angels back when, but the fact was they had chosen to become sluts in Hell and had taken money for sex. Hell was loaded with fallen angels who had lost their once-upon-a-time heavenly status for Satan's cause. And they had allowed themselves to be reduced to thieves, smugglers, money lenders, drunkards, dope users, and whores. Unlike her sister Mili, Mardie had no pity for the two dead angels. They were bitches who'd squandered their inheritances.

For some reason, Mardie thought of Hugh Everett III once again. She liked him. She liked his big laugh and whacky occupations. Her favorite one—and easily the most startling—was his long stint at the Pentagon where he and a think tank full of colleagues as brilliant as him had run collateral damage scenarios. How many civilians were likely to be killed in various atomic war strikes. Human carnage reduced to math. And who said you'd never have a use for Algebra? Some goddamned pessimist who never worked for the military.

Hugh Everett had opted to remain on the parallel world he had entered chasing the murderous alternate Hugh Everett. After that Everett died—of the several bullets Hugh had shot into his back—that parallel world was suddenly short one quantum physicist. Hugh had stayed. He reunited with his wife in that new world, and his daughter, and he'd joined his son's band. His boy Mark had spent a lot of time during his life asking people to hug him. When his father met up with him and asked for his forgiveness, Mark found out that his dad gave pretty good hugs.

Mardie had tried to outdrink Hugh Everett one night when he was still in Hell, and he had bested her by a long shot. She developed a little crush on the big man that night and had learned to share his fondness for Crown Royal Perfect Manhattans. She wondered if he was truly visiting Albert Einstein unannounced?

She couldn't believe that Hugh would deliberately avoid Satan. He probably just didn't want to bother him. Mardie was sure though that Lucifer would be glad to see him. She knew that *she* would be delighted to see him. Late hours. Binge drinking. Suggestive banter. By God, that would almost be as good as carousing as a young flirt back on Earth again.

Mili began to study the bodies of the slain angels. She pulled on latex gloves then reached down and checked inside the empty abdominal cavity where the second angel's female organs had been cut out. The cuts appeared reckless compared to the smooth surgical slit that had opened her throat. Mili didn't take time to consider why female angels would have uteruses, relegating that question to metaphysical pursuits of doctrinaire Catholic purists like Saint Thomas Aquinas who had seriously contemplated how many angels could dance on the head of a pin.

Had Jack the Ripper been in a hurry? Or just didn't care? For the first time Mili realized why Jack had been designated the Ripper. While he had meticulously cut the hookers' throats, draining away their lives, he had carelessly—perhaps even deliberately—slashed their bellies open to tear away their womanhood. Jack the Ripper, indeed.

Mili's mobile phone rang. She jumped. She pulled off a glove and fished it out of her purse. It was Lucifer. His face looked rested and happy. She answered.

"Hello, dear. How are you?"

"Hello, sweet," he responded. "I am doing rather well considering our house is in ashes and I'm here at the kibbutz without you."

"I miss you. How are the children?"

"Settling in happily. Little Mardie talked Sriracha into trying some vegetables. And he's thrilled to be playing with kids his own age for the first time ever. In fact, he's so occupied with the games and the competitions that he seems to have lost his inclination to incinerate everything."

Mili smiled and felt a pang of loneliness for her children.

"And what are *you* doing to keep busy, Lu?"

"I've begun helping with some kibbutz chores," the Devil answered. "Picking fruit in the orchards. Weeding vegetable plots. Helping set up irrigation systems. All of it is quite enjoyable, really. And I am happy to be outside enjoying the fresh air and blue skies. Bloody miracle those. Ben-Gurion works hard and talks endlessly. Moshe Dayan works twice as hard and was amazed to find some artifacts in a field near the kibbutz dating back to folks who lived here before the Jews."

"*Before* the Jews?" Mili asked surprised. "Who might they have been?"

"Moshe's not sure. He thinks maybe Mormons. You know, the self-proclaimed descendants of the lost tribes of Israel. At any rate, Moshe is thrilled with the objects he found."

Mili smiled. She was happy for Dayan. Even happy for the Mormons.

"What is it like to have all those young people running around?" she asked.

"I'm finding it quite charming," he told her. "Most of the kids are no more than five or six, and new ones are being born every day. It's not an issue yet, but as dating and marriage catch on, it's going to cause a major upheaval down here. We'll have the damned, and we'll also have the children of the damned living in actual human bodies right alongside the Hellions, with entirely different requirements for each group. It's a future headache without a doubt."

"You'll deal with it, darling," Mili assured him.

"Thanks, doll," Lucifer replied savoring the compliment. "How are you doing with our *present* headache? Namely Jack the Ripper."

"Well, sad to say, Mardie and I are at the temporary morgue viewing the bodies of the two Sekhmet demons who were Jack's first victims. They've transformed into their heavenly bodies."

Lucifer's face went very solemn.

"They've turned back into angels?"

"Yes."

"How do they look?" Satan asked.

"Completely beautiful. Eternal. Perfect. As if they should have lived forever."

The Devil looked at Mili and appeared lost for words.

"Would you turn your phone camera toward the bodies?" Satan asked. "I am sure I must know both angels."

"Is that something you really want me to do?" Mili asked.

"No," Lucifer answered. "But I think it's important. No matter how foul the angels allowed themselves to become after being driven from Heaven, I owe them a nod and a farewell for their loyalty and their bravery."

Mili held the camera on the two bodies and then slowly panned up to show the angels' faces. And their wounds. It was awful, and she could only imagine how tragic it was for Lucifer, seeing the dead faces of his comrades. The once fearless companions who'd followed him into the breech against Jehovah.

Mili looked at the monitor on her phone. The screen was dark.

Lucifer had gone.

CHAPTER TEN

"I need to go to the kibbutz," Mili told Mardie after they left the refrigeration unit.

"Was Lucifer bummed seeing the bodies of the angels?" Mardie asked.

"He hung up."

Mardie shook her head.

"I need to see him, and I miss the kids," Mili said. "Want to come along?"

"No," Mardie answered. "But thanks. Bowles texted me that the Good News Club would like me to help track down whoever doctored last night's reenactment script."

Pfot had the Volvo waiting. He greeted Mill and Mardie and opened the passenger doors for them. Getting into the driver's seat, he asked where they wanted to go.

"Mardie is heading home, Pfot," Mili replied. "And I'd like a ride to the kibbutz."

"Yes, ma'am," Pfotenhauer replied.

"Also," Mardie added, "if you can handle driving back from the kibbutz after dropping Mili, Pfot, I'd like you to be my guest tonight at the Good News Club. They're doing some new and controversial material, *Abraham Sacrifices Isaac*. I'd like your opinion."

"Well, thank you, Miss Mardie," Pfotenhauer replied. "That's very kind of you and all, but those plays remind me way too much of working for the mob. This man tricks that one. That man kills this one. Then the boss gets angry and kills everybody."

"You're spot on, Pfot," Mardie said. "And that why I really want you to see the new reeneactment. How would you feel about a home-cooked meal at my house first? Say a nice shepherd's pie with a couple of Guinness stouts to wash it down?"

"I accept," Pfot said instantly. "I could watch *any* play with a stomach full of shepherd's pie."

"Then we're on," Mardie said. "I have almost everything I need for dinner, but I would like to add some salad fixings. Do you suppose you could fetch a few fresh things back with you from the kibbutz?"

"Certainly," Pfot answered.

"Great! Why don't you come by my house around six o'clock?"

"Is that enough time to dine before the play?" Pfot asked.

"Aye, it is," Mardie answered. "And even better, it's enough time to eat *and* get to the Club early enough to have another drink!"

✳ ✳ ✳

Lucifer greeted Mili with a hug and a long kiss when she arrived at the kibbutz. He was wearing blue shorts, a gray T-shirt, and natural-colored leather sandals. Mili had on a new blue-and-white striped summer dress and white flip-flops. She had begun replacing all the clothes that she and the family had lost in the house fire.

"Let's go to the cafeteria and get some lemonade," he said. "Local lemons. Ice cold. Made with lots of sugar. And we can enjoy it right there because air conditioning has just been installed."

"That's wonderful!" Mili declared. "Why the sudden upgrade?"

"A generous donor who you might know anted up the money as a gift to the kibbutz."

"Who would that be?"

"Idi Amin," the Devil replied. "I told him that I needed money for a special charity and he was happy to offer it."

"Just like that?" Mili asked suspiciously.

"Almost," Satan said and winked. "I promised him that I would lift the ban on his bowling in the championships."

"Even though he bribed the alley attendants to rig the pin-set software so that his pins fell down without even being hit?"

"Even though."

"I don't like that man," Mili said in a mean tone.

"You don't have to like him. You just have to like his air conditioning."

"I don't know," Mili resisted. "Isn't he also the psychopath who kept the heads of his enemies in a freezer?"

"Maybe."

"Maybe?"

Mili scowled at her husband.

"They weren't all his enemies," Satan replied.

"*That* falls pretty short, Lucifer Morningstar."

"Yep," the Devil responded. "I would have frozen their hands, too."

Mili stopped and stared at Lucifer.

"This is not a playful topic."

Satan looked embarrassed.

"You're right," he apologized sincerely. "I think that seeing the dead angels sort of screwed up my sensibilities."

"Did you recognize them?"

"Of course, I did."

"I was surprised to see that they were female," Mili said. "And appeared to have reproductive organs that had been removed."

Satan nodded.

"I think that Elohim originally wanted the angels to have children. They were fond of saying that only bearing a child taught someone how to love unconditionally."

Mili was struck by Lucifer's explanation. In her own life she felt huge affection and love for him and her sister Mardie. But with her children she gave her whole heart without reservation. She didn't even think about it. That's just how it was.

She looked at Satan's face as they walked. Despite his sadness over the murdered angels, he appeared calm and content. He'd only been on the kibbutz a couple of days, but she could already see its beneficial effects on him.

"You like it here, don't you, sweet?" she asked.

"I do. It is fresh. Untainted. Pure. Also, the people are quite wonderful. Not just Ben-Gurion and Dayan. *Everyone*. They get along and they even spend time together when the day's chores are done. On Saturdays they take a day of rest and there's singing and dancing, and it seems like everyone plays an instrument."

"You witnessed that?"

"I was *part* of that! Yesterday I danced and sang songs. Everyone gathered in the parking area in front of the dining hall. Little Mardie and Sriracha danced and sang, too. They did great." The Devil smiled remembering. "Unfortunately, Sriracha relieved himself behind one chap's set of kettle drums and they burned up. They had lambskin heads, so it smelled like it was dinnertime for a while. Then it was. Sriracha tried lamb roasted in garlic and butter. He looked at me with big questioning eyes and asked me if he was eating a little baby lamb. I said that he was. He said yum."

Lucifer held open the door to the dining hall for Mili. She stepped inside. The air inside felt cool and perfect.

"Wow, this is nice."

"Have a seat anywhere, and I'll get us some lemonade."

Mili sat at a large table. There were some folks happily cooling off nearby, and many of them waved cordially when she smiled at them.

Cafeterias always brought back fond memories of her years dining at Scotland Yard. The fare hadn't been all that appealing, but then what British food ever was? It was the camaraderie that she had loved. Chatting with her colleagues. Especially other homicide inspectors. Sharing cases, clues, and solutions. Someone almost inevitably smuggled in a flask of whiskey to share. She wished she had that kind of professional fellowship in Hell.

She thought again that there was no police force down here. But after meeting Inspector Abberline, she realized that there were probably other Scotland Yard officers in Hell. Whatever sins they had brought them here, they had likely been models of law and order as federal police. The best of them could make a splendid police force here. And with all the changes in Hell—rape, assault, murder—Mili determined then and there to talk to Lucifer about establishing a formal law enforcement agency.

Satan brought two tall chilled glasses of lemonade. He put one in front of Mili and took the chair next to her. He smiled at her, happy and content.

"Thank you for coming today, love," he told her. "I would like you to consider the possibility of all of us just staying on here at the kibbutz."

"I can't think of any objections at all," Mili responded, sipping at her tangy, sugary drink. "It feels like family."

Satan smiled and reached over to squeeze Mili's hand.

"It's also a pivotal time here," Lucifer said. "The kibbutz is terraforming things down here at a significant rate. And I've been thinking again of the vast changes to Hell's demograhics in the future. As both Hellions and their adult children marry and have babies, it is only a matter of time before we will need schools and universities. A ton of new industries to provide jobs. Maybe even churches and synagogues."

Mili choked on her lemonade. The Devil got up and pounded her back until she could breathe again.

"Let's not get religious," she gasped.

"No kidding," her husband said sympathetically. "Almost killed you."

✳ ✳ ✳

Mardie picked up her chiming iPhone from the bed stand. It was Mili calling at 4:14 a.m.

"Hello, Mil," she managed to whisper.

"Mardie, I am *so* sorry to bother you, but Trump just called me and said that another Sekhmet has been murdered."

Mardie sat up wide awake.

"Impossible! The second one was murdered only two days ago."

"I know. This time the killer mutilated the Sekhmet even worse than the others. You don't have to look, but I need you to go and help Trump keep the crime scene intact again. He and a couple of Lucifer's aides are there, but I can't get there until I can get a ride there from the kibbutz. The murder took place on Lubomir Street, just a block down from the last murder on Novak."

"I'll go," Mardie said. "Please call Trump back and tell him I'll be there as soon as I get a taxi to pick me up."

"Thanks, Mardie."

"De nada," Mardie replied and pressed the *Off* button. De nada, my ass, she thought. It *wasn't* nothing to get up in the middle of the night and head off to a murder scene. At least Bowles hadn't stayed over, or she never would have been able to get out of bed.

A taxi pulled up to the main kibbutz building twenty minutes after she called. Mardie could barely see it. Its headlights were off. Its backlights were off. She walked up to the driver's window. It was open. She leaned down and told him that all his lights were off. Not *off* he responded. Gone. Mardie thought about that a moment and then opened the passenger door and got in the backseat. How lucky she was that Pfotenhauer usually provided her rides. The cabbie started the meter and off they went.

Mardie thought she recognized him. Tall man. Thin wiseass face. Cloud of white curls.

"Are you Kurt Vonnegut?" she asked.

"No," the driver answered. "Vonnegut's in Heaven. I'm Kilgore Trout."

Mardie was completely surprised.

"You were in a lot of his novels," Mardie responded. "I thought you were just made up."

"I should be so lucky," Kilgore replied. "Then I wouldn't be down here."

Can't argue with that, Mardie thought.

"Why is Vonnegut in Heaven and you're not?"

"Might as well ask Captain Ahab why Melville is in Heaven and he's not."

"Does that happen a lot?" Mardie asked. "I mean, where the author is sainted and his character is damned?"

"Only if the character was a real person."

"Okay, got that," Mardie replied. "Are there a lot of authors in Hell?"

"A lot of the good ones are. Hemingway is here. So is Scott Fitzgerald. Even big-hearted Philip Roth is here. On the other hand, Miller, Pinter, and Kosinski are all in Heaven."

"Jerzy Kosinski is in Heaven?" Mardie cried. "No way!"

"Well, he is."

"Have you met any of the writers who wound up down here?" Mardie asked.

"I have autographed firsts by Papa, Scotty, and Phil. Wanna buy one?"

"*Old Man and the Sea*?" Mardie asked.

"Sheesh lareesh!" Trout exclaimed. "Everyone asks about that overrated piece. How about a signed first of Steinbeck's *Grapes of Wrath*? I can get both Henry Fonda and John Carradine to sign it, too."

"Who is John Carradine?"

"Never mind. I'll get Ward Bond to sign."

"Actually, just Steinbeck would be great."

"Got a credit card?"

"If you drop the book at Lucifer's main office and tell them it's for his sister-in-law, they'll pay you without a question."

Kilgore was impressed.

"Can do, and thank you, ma'am."

Five minutes later, Trout dropped Mardie off well before the crowd gathered at the crime scene in New Babylon.

Mardie paid the fare in cash and made one last request.

"I'll also take any books about you, or by you, provided you autograph them."

"Bless you," Trout responded, a big smile on his face. "You're an angel."

No, I'm not an angel, Mardie thought and stepped out of the cab. She looked at the crime scene up the street. Especially not tonight.

CHAPTER ELEVEN

The crowd surrounding the dead Sekhmet parted to let Mardie through. Trump was there, wearing black dress slacks, a white shirt, and black Florsheims. He looked crisp and professional.

"Hello, Trump," Mardie greeted him. "I'll bet you look a Hell of a lot better than the corpse under that overcoat." She nodded at the covered body at their feet.

"Good morning, Miss Mardie," Trump replied. "I try to look presentable," he replied modestly.

"Well, I appreciate that, young man. What were you doing when this got called in?"

"Finishing a date."

Mardie wasn't familiar with that expression, but it wasn't too hard to guess what Trump meant.

"Luckily we were at my place, so I could get here quickly," Trump added.

"After a lot of hair combing, I would guess," Mardie said with a grin.

Trump kept a straight face.

"Who reported the murder?" Mardie asked.

"A gentleman who was heading home after a night out with his friends. He found the body, laid his overcoat over it, then called Lucifer's office."

"What was his name?"

"He said it was Fulbright."

"Did Mr. Fulbright explain how he happened to be wearing a heavy overcoat in the middle
of the night?" Mardie asked. "In the middle of Hell? A bit unusual considering it was probably ninety-five degrees out."

"Sorry, ma'am," Trump apologized. "I didn't ask."

"It's not an issue, dear boy," Mardie said reassuringly. "It's just that *anybody* walking around Hell wearing a big overcoat draws my attention."

"Concerned about flashers?" Trump guessed.

"Hell, no. I love a good laugh as much as the next person. But when I see someone wearing a coat down here, I suspect it's to conceal a knife, or a gun, or a club."

Trump gazed at Mardie impressed by her suspicious nature.

"Didn't you used to write poems?" he asked.

"Yes. How would you know that?"

"I remember Lucifer reading them. Quite a long time ago now."

"Sumbitch!" Mardie exclaimed. "Did you read them, too?"

"No. The Devil was interrupted. The eventual outcome of which was a temper tantrum."

"And he burned the shit out of them?"

"I'm afraid so."

She had once lived to write poems, Mardie remembered. But her life had become so busy since her twin Milicent had come to Hell that composing verse had become passé. She didn't really mind. She had written her hard knock poems out of loneliness and despair. She wasn't subject to either of those now. How much different her circumstances had become. Out with the tortured soul. In with the tortured bodies.

"Do you want to view the victim?" Trump asked.

"Absolutely not!" Mardie said vehemently. "I'm only here because Mili asked me to join you to ensure that the body is undisturbed. Pfotenhauer is here in the city so she is taking a taxi from the kibbutz."

"Right-O," Trump said. "It's not an issue. Things are sorted for the time being."

"Yes, except for one thing," Mardie replied.

Trump looked at her, a questioning expression on his face.

"A nice hot cup of coffee would sort of round out this whole keeping-tabs-on-the-body stakeout."

Mardie gazed at Trump until he realized that was a hint.

"No problem," he piped up. "How would you like that coffee, Ms. Wickett?"

"With lots of Irish."

※ ※ ※

Mili arrived a little after seven o'clock. Dawn was more subdued in New Babylon than in the country. And the air was stale, not sweet. Welcome back to the real Hell, she thought. Mili greeted Mardie and Trump and told them that cab driver couldn't get here any sooner because of all the trucks on the road.

Mardie frowned.

"I have never seen a single truck on that road," she contradicted Mili.

"Yes? Well, that was then, and this is now," Mili answered. "The highway was full of eighteen-wheelers from the kibbutz. They leave early hauling fresh produce to the city. Each cab had a name stenciled on its door. Menachem Begin. Anne Frank. Simon Peres. Teddy Kollek. You get the idea."

Mardie frowned again.

"How could you read all those names?"

"The driver passed every truck."

Mili studied her sister's face. Mardie seemed uncharacteristically grumpy.

"Have you been drinking?" she asked her.

"Only coffee."

Mili looked at Trump. He looked away.

"How many *coffees* have you had?" Mili asked her sister.

"Not nearly enough."

Mili glanced at Trump again. He held up four fingers. Mili shook her head and walked over to the body.

"Overcoat?" she said surprised. "A heavy outer coat?"

"Miss Mardie raised that issue, too," Trump responded. "No one saw the person who covered the corpse. But it belongs to the man who called this in."

"Name?"

"Fulbright."

"First name?"

"He didn't offer one," Trump answered.

"No matter," Mili said. "If it was the Ripper, he would have just lied anyway. Same as he did at the time of the first murder when he called himself Proxmire. *And* he didn't give you a first name then either. Do you know, by the way, that in the old days first names were referred to as Christian names?

"And back then most of them were. I always had a great time watching the crusty old desk sergeants at the Yard trying to book ladies and gents who were Jews or Muslims. They had no idea how to answer when they were asked what their *Christian* names were. Ha! And then, of course, the Yard chaps would get impatient at the bewildered folks and snap 'Speak up!'"

Trump grinned. He loved Mrs. Morningstar. He was sure that she was the brightest and wittiest person in Hell.

"*My* first name is Milicent, Trump," she said. "Don't know if you were aware of that. People call me Mili which is fine. But since my sister's name is Mardell everyone seems to mix us up. Mili and Mardie. I actually cannot figure out why. One look at my sister's porn star figure should make it a snap to tell the difference between us."

Trump blushed.

Mili smiled.

"I like a man who can still blush, Trump. I was going to use *your* first name just now, dear boy, but then I realized that I don't know it."

"Actually, I don't have a first name, ma'am," Trump explained. "My parents thought that a historically provocative surname like Trump would do me well enough."

"It *is* a strong name," Mili agreed. "Especially given its history in card games. And in the Oval Office."

Trump grinned.

"I think that's what they had in mind."

"Quite," Mili said. She looked at Trump's handsome features and his full head of immaculately groomed blonde hair.

"Pardon my snooping," she told him. "But how did you come to find yourself working for my husband down here?"

"I was a sailor in World War II. A radioman assigned to a landing support craft built to participate in the invasions of the Japanese-held islands. I was a devout Christian and took a lot of abuse from the crew for separating myself from their bad habits—drinking, smoking, gambling, and whoring. On the way to the Pacific fleet, our skipper made all of us jump in the ocean over the Marianas Trench, some 36,000 feet deep."

Mili could see that despite Trump's calm narration, his face had become anxiety ridden as he told his story. Small drops of perspiration appeared on his forehead.

"The captain said we'd tell our kids about it someday. He tossed a rope ladder over the side of the boat for us to climb back up. When it was my turn, a sailor named Mulke began pulling it up. I yelled to the captain, and he ordered Mulke to lower it again. That same night when

I went to relieve Mulke of guard duty on the stern of the boat, I hit him in the face with the butt of my rifle and knocked him overboard. I never heard a sound.

"No one knew what happened to Mulke except me. I was never sorry that I did it. After the war I died in a car crash in my hometown of Sioux City, Iowa. I was an unrepentant murderer and wound up down here. Because I knew shorthand, your husband added me to his office crew. Eventually, I became the staff member who did most of his personal errands. Quickly and without mistakes."

"I like you, Trump," Mili said, appreciating the young man's candor. "And just for the record, I think you did the right thing in settling up with that Mulke chap."

"Thank you, ma'am." Trump's face looked sad, however. "I have to say though, that my actions caused me to spend eternity apart from my father and my mother. I am sure they went to Heaven. I, of course, did not."

"What church did you belong too?"

"The Lutheran Church-Missouri Synod."

"I know that one," Mili acknowledged. "Denomination full of people convinced that they are the only ones going to Heaven."

"That's actually the Southern Baptists, ma'am," Trump said.

Mili chuckled.

"Well, thank Heaven we can keep *them* busy down here with reenactments."

"May I tell you a secret?" Trump's face looked very serious.

"Cross my heart and hope to die."

"Your husband was the one who rewrote the reenactment script for *Abraham Sacrifices Isaac*."

"That little shit!" Mili spit out hating Lucifer's cleverness.

"He based it on abstruse middle ages commentaries on the Islamic Qu'ran. They offer quite a different take on Isaac's fate than the standard Qu'ran verses."

Mili scowled.

"How did he ever get the born agains to go along with an altered script?"

"How does *anyone* get persuaded down here?"

"They took bribes?" Mili said aghast.

"They took *gifts*."

"For free." Mili was disgusted.

"I think that defines a gift."

"You'd make a good defense lawyer, Trump."

"I wanted to be a pastor. But I didn't live long enough."

"Sorry," Mili commiserated. "But I am happy that you're down here with us."

Trump blushed again.

Mardie reinserted herself into the conversation.

"I'm glad that you two have had a bonding opportunity," she said sarcastically. "And the only reason I am interrupting is to tell you that I am going back to bed."

"I'll call a cab," Trump offered.

"No need," Mardie said slurring her words. She looked at Mili. "Pfotenhauer went home after last night's re-enactment. I'll call him for a ride."

"He's probably still sleeping," Mili told her.

"I can wake him up."

"That's not what I am concerned about," Mili answered. "I'm worried about you finding him in your *tired* condition."

"Mrs. Morningstar?" Trump spoke up. "May I escort Ms. Wickett?"

"Yes. Thank you so much."

Mardie gave Mili a peck on the cheek and took Trump's arm. They headed for the street.

Mili was finally able to turn her attention to the body covered by the overcoat. She took hold of the collar of the London Fog-style coat—gray and heavy—and slowly lifted it off the cadaver. She laid it on the street and looked at the naked Sekhmet. She held her breath. Then breathed out slowly, murmuring, "Oh, God. Oh, God."

The woman's throat had been slit. She and the street were stained with blood. Both of her breasts had been sheared off. Her vulva, vagina, ovaries, and uterus had been removed. Jagged cuts had ripped open her flesh and blood covered the Sekhmet's thighs. As bad as all of that was, the worst sight was the Sekhmet's face. It was not there. The ears were cut off. The nose was sheared away revealing the nostril holes in the skull. And the eyes were gouged out leaving blood-filled pools. Then the killer had flayed what remained of the Sekhmet's face and pulled off her entire scalp.

Mili stepped back without realizing that she had done so. In her thirty-seven years working Scotland Yard's Homicide Desk, she had never seen anything this horrific. Three Sekhmets had now been murdered in eight days and each body had been more mutilated than the last. This was truly the work of the same killer who had performed these kinds of monstrous depravities on the London prostitutes a hundred year and thirty years ago.

Trump returned in a few minutes and stood next to Mili. He stared silently at the corpse.

"Christ Almighty, Trump," she murmured. "Who could do this kind of thing?"

Trump only shook his head.

"Let's get the poor thing off the street and into the freezer," Mili ordered. "I want a physician familiar with Scotland Yard autopsy procedures to work on the cadaver. I need vaginal tissues checked for foreign DNA samples. And I want that coat checked for DNA as well." She gazed for a moment at the ruined face and body of the dead Sekhmet. She spoke to Trump again. "Times like this, I not only fantasize about dismembering such a perpetrator head to toe, I feel frustrated that no punishment exists here in Hell suitable for the viciousness and violence the killer used on his victims."

Trump kept his eyes on the corpse, but spoke softly to Mili.

"Vigilantes exist in *all* places, Mrs. Morningstar. Avenging innocent victims."

Mili looked at Trump. He turned his head and looked at her.

"What exactly are you saying?" she asked him.

"I think you know what I am saying, ma'am," Trump responded. "Men of honor dwell down here, and when a situation demands it, they take justice into their own hands, visiting the evil done by such men as Jack the Ripper upon their own flesh."

Mili gazed into Trump's eyes for a long time. He did not look away. She finally spoke again.

"Is there a Yard inspector named Abberline in the group you describe?"

"I may only answer that if you join the fellowship and sanction its activities."

Mili squinted at Trump.

"Activities?"

"Removing fingers, toes, hands, and feet. Administering piercings, cuts, and punctures. Detaching eyes, ears, and tongues. Pulling up muscles and cutting them. Breaking bones from the neck to the ankle." Trump paused. "Want to hear more?"

"So, it's torture?"

"No. It's *just desserts*. We keep the evil-doers alive for as long as they last without food or water."

"And then you just let them die?"

Trump shook his head slowly.

"No. When death is imminent the person's crimes are read aloud in front of his or her face.

A sentence of death is pronounced. And then the individual is shot between the eyes."

"You have guns?"

"All kinds of guns."

"Guns are illegal in Hell."

"For all but a few of us they are. We obtain ours with your husband's permission."

"But if you can obtain them legitimately, then I would think that virtually anyone could obtain them *illegitimately*."

"Very likely. But I only need answer for the guns that Satan allows us to possess. And use."

Mili shook her head. These activities went completely against the moral and professional training she held dear. She shook her head.

"I can't do it."

"I understand, Mrs. Morningstar," Trump said sympathetically.

"How do you keep your sweet baby face?" Mili asked staring at him.

"By lying."

Mili frowned.

"Beg your pardon?"

"Everything I've told you about myself is a fabrication for consumption down here. Only Lucifer knows my true identity and *that* is why he asked me to work for him. Most people think that I only exist in a book. But the book was real and the story was true. If you know the author Oscar Wilde, then you know who I am."

Mili covered her mouth with her hands, then spoke in a whisper.

"Dorian Gray."

CHAPTER TWELVE

Mardie was fixing a late breakfast for herself and Mili who had stayed the night. Her twin sat at the kitchen table reviewing the autopsy results and the lab tests she had ordered yesterday. The last murdered Sekhmet had been sexually assaulted. The DNA recovered from the attacker's fluids matched DNA samples removed from the overcoat left at the scene the previous night. Everything conclusively pointed to the same criminal who had raped and murdered the first two Sekhmets. Unfortunately, Mili had no idea who that criminal was.

"I'm a wreck," Mardie said, cooking eggs in one skillet and bacon in another. She and Mili had already had black tea and were working on refills.

"Not enough sleep?" Mili asked.

"Not enough bacon. Though I'd also love to get a nap in after we eat. Every time I think of you and your family living on the kibbutz, I crave bacon."

"We don't eat bacon there."

"Makes it twice as weird."

"You know," Mili mused, "I've had a craving for bacon lately as well. In fact, I've had a few cravings. Pickles. Potato chips. Cookies."

Mardie looked at her sister.

"Are you pregnant?" she asked.

Mili laughed.

"Of course not. I'd know it if I was PG don't you think?"

"Eggs scrambled and bacon done crisp?" Mardie asked. "And when did you have your last period?"

"Yes, please," Mili answered. "And Hellions don't have periods, remember?"

"Oh, right. And Hellions don't have babies either, do they?" Mardie asked rhetorically.

"I'm not pregnant," Mili insisted. "Okay?"

"Okay. Just checking."

Mardie served Mili her eggs and bacon, along with some hash browns fried up with onions and red peppers, two slices of buttered wheat toast, quince jelly, and a bowl of fresh apricots. Mili popped one of the apricots in her mouth and checked out Mardie's short sleeve blouse. It was white with red polka dots, and she was wearing it with red shorts. Mardie noticed Mili staring at her outfit.

"What? You don't like it?" she asked.

"Ever see the American comedian Lucille Ball on the telly?"

"No."

"Then just eat. This food looks wonderful, thank you."

"Welcome."

Mardie served herself, then sat down and began eating. She only had scrambled eggs and bacon. She skipped the potatoes and the fruit. Unlike her sister, she ate to live, not lived to eat. Though she did have this big thing for bacon right now.

"So how did Pfot like the reenactment the other night?" Mili asked her. "Too much like his mob life after all?"

"Apparently not. He enjoyed it. He did say that he found it hard to watch Abraham sacrifice Isaac, but he understood that a pretender could not be in the lineage of Jesus."

"I found out, by the way," Mili said, "who the despicable party was who messed with the script."

"I still can't believe someone got away with that," Mardie said shaking her head. "Where were the bleedin' Evangelicals when we needed them?"

"They took bribes."

"I don't believe that!" Mardie protested. "Those are devout Christians we're talking about."

Mili glanced at Mardie and tried not to smile.

"All right. Call them *gifts* then. The fact is, my husband rewrote the reenactment and the players went along with it. I can't tell you who squealed on him, but I got it from someone in the know."

"Trump," Mardie said.

Mili scowled.

"How could you *possibly* know it was him?" she snapped.

"You spent all yesterday morning together at the crime scene. And your rudeness now at being caught simply confirms that I'm right."

Mili finished her breakfast, then spoke up again.

"I'm sorry," she apologized. "Of course, it was Trump. I am pissed off at my spouse and I took it out on you."

"Classic passive-aggressive behavior," Mardie commented.

"Which is not like me," Mili replied defending herself.

"It is when you're pregnant."

"You can remember?"

"I can't forget it. You get really rude."

"Forgive me?"

"Only if you get a pregnancy test. I imagine they have kits for that sort of thing at the drug store or supermarket. Even in *this* piece-of-shite city. And if for some reason they don't, ask Lucifer to pick you up a couple at the kibbutz infirmary. The Jews there are multiplying like pagans."

"May I have more bacon?" Mili asked refusing to acknowledge her sister's teasing.

"Sure. More eggs, too? Extra toast?"

"Just bacon, please."

"How many pieces?"

"How many will fit in the pan?"

Mardie got up and looked at the skillet.

"Maybe twelve."

"I'd like twelve pieces, please."

Mardie put a hand on her hip and stared at her sister. Mili stared back at her, offended at Mardie's intimidating posture.

"It's only forty-three calories per slice and no one gets fatter down here anyway," Mili said.

"It's not *you* I'm worried about," Mardie responded. "I don't want to be blamed for single-handedly depleting the porcus population down here."

Mili cast a withering look at Mardie who just grinned and began putting the bacon slices in the pan.

"Can I run something by you?" Mili asked, refilling her tea cup and Mardie's.

"Sure."

Mili added a cascade of cream to her tea and six teaspoons of sugar.

"Trump is reviewing Shapeshifter profiles in Lucifer's office," she told Mardie. "He's looking for a half-dozen likely candidates to stakeout the streets tonight as Sekhmet prostitutes. The actual Sekhmet streetwalkers who ply their trade in the area will be there, too. Both real and faux hookers will be waiting for the appearance of the Ripper.

"Now, my question. Do you think we should supply knives to both groups of Sekhmets as protection against Mad Jack? That's Lucifer's plan, but I am not sure it's wise to do so."

Mardie flipped the bacon strips and answered.

"The only consideration is whether or not a knife will be of any help. Jack the Ripper is strong and can apparently slit a female's throat in a heartbeat. How does one defend against that? Flash a knife while your throat is gushing and your knickers are being pulled down? Not likely.

I suppose though that a Sekhmet in that situation could still put a knife in his ribs. Better late than never."

"If things progress that quickly," Mili answered, "sticking Jack in the ribs would just guarantee a final reprisal. The real protection for the Sekhmets—both prostitutes and Shapeshifters—is *the ability of other persons to intervene instantly*. Trump and a handful of his comrades will be in close proximity to all of the Sekhmets we're using for bait—pardon that expression—and *they* will be armed for close encounters with the killer. Guns, knives, and billy clubs. If they get their hands on the Ripper they will probably kill him on the spot."

Mardie used a fork to lift the bacon out of the pan and put it on a plate. She pressed a paper towel against the slices to soak up some of the grease, then brought the bacon over to the table and set it in front of Mili.

"I vote no knives for the ladies," she said as she sat down.

"Thanks ever so much for the bacon," Mili replied. "And I agree with you. No knives."

"Make sure then," Mardie cautioned, "that whoever encounters Jack will have help almost instantaneously. Otherwise another Sekhmet will be dead before he can be stopped."

Mili nodded and ate her bacon. How unfortunate for the poor pig that his position in the food chain was such that he could easily be singled out for slaughter. Just like Sekhmets at this particular time. Tragic to be either the pig or the prostitute, though personally she'd rather take her chances protecting herself as a Sekhmet than as a walking barrel of bacon.

✳ ✳ ✳

Dusk was giving way to dark and a dozen Sekhmets walked the Ripper District, which was what the prostitutes called the killing zone. Six of them were demon Sekhmets selling sex. The other six were Shapeshifters from the Devil's own trusted list of ne'er-do-wells. They were minions he had picked and paid well for various skin-changing tasks in the past. He was using them again tonight as faux Sekhmets. Their talents were legendary and their accomplishments renowned.

Lucifer's favorite of the lot was E. Ran Wagner, a demon with profound thespian instincts. Once when Will Shakespeare had paid the Devil to provide a ghost of Hamlet's father at the Globe Theater on opening night, Wagner had gotten the role and done a smashing job. He was so good, in fact, that when the players and the audience realized that a *real* spirit was playing the dead king's ghost, absolutely *everyone* shit their pants and ran for the streets. Contemporary musings about the event deigned it the Most Unusual Theater Opening that season, and applauded the unknown Geist for generating the Most Offensive Audience Reaction ever.

The Sekhmets spread out around a small park near where the murders had occurred, posting themselves in various alleys where they could conduct their business. None of them seemed nervous, and Trump and his vigilantes were outright confident. Mili didn't recognize any of the men accompanying him. They were a rough-looking crew, outfitted in canvas work pants, plaid shirts, suspenders, and hobnail boots. Unshaved and unwashed, they had beady eyes and suspicious demeanors. All of them looked like the kinds of unsavory characters industrial capitalists had once employed to disrupt public protests and break up union strikes.

Trump had told her earlier that each man carried a weapon of his own personal preference—knives, clubs, cricket bats, hammers, and chains. Mili suspected they had guns, too, tucked into their belts and covered by their shirttails. Or tucked into shoulder holsters. She suspected that Trump himself had a secret gun. He surely wasn't planning to face the Ripper mano a mano without tilting the odds in his favor. And that meant carrying a gun. Fine with her. Shoot the fucking bastard. With a canon.

Trump and Mili stood in a corner of the small park where a gas lamp lit up a bench for idlers and a sandbox for youngsters. Mili didn't see any families present, but Trump nodded toward a man seated on the bench. He was a tall slim man dressed like a laborer. He was wearing a white long sleeve shirt, blue work pants, and a black leather cap with a bill. The man had placed a tool bag on the bench next to him. He rolled a cigarette and smoked it. He repeated this again and again over the next three hours, littering the grass with cigarette butts. Shortly before midnight Trump whispered in Mili's ear.

"It's got to be the Ripper. What other blighter would sit and wait like that? I'm going to confront him."

"Don't be wrong," Mili told him.

"I'll wait here for five minutes," Trump replied. "Please go to my chaps and direct their attention to the man on the bench."

Mili quietly located the vigilantes posted in alleys, standing behind hedges, and hunched down beside parked cars. They followed her back to the park just in time to see Trump approach the seated man. They drew out their weapons and crossed the park.

The man on the bench watched Trump. He reached into his satchel and stood up. He held a long-barrel .45 Colt revolver in his hand and fired it directly into Trump's chest. Trump fell to the ground. The vigilantes ran for the shooter. He reached into his bag again. He faced the men with a six-shooter in *each* hand and began firing.

The man shot both revolvers nonstop. One of Trump's men was hit in the face. He threw his arms wide and fell. Another was hit in the abdomen. He cried out, "O Lord, save me!" and crumpled. Two more men crashed to the ground with bullets in their faces and chests. A last man was hit in the neck and fell. All of Trump's men lay dead or wounded. The shooter pulled a handful of bullet cartridges out of his tool bag and began reloading his pistols.

Suddenly Trump jumped to his feet and as quick as God's judgment pulled a small pistol out of his coat pocket and aimed it at the shooter. The man backed away as Trump fired. He was struck in the shoulder and cried out in pain. Blood exploded onto his shirt. He jumped at Trump and smashed his temple with the butt of his revolver. Trump staggered, then fell backwards onto the grass.

The shooter grabbed his bag and escaped into the shadows. Mili ran over and knelt by Trump. He was unconscious and breathing heavily. He'd recover from the blow to the head. She was more concerned that he'd been shot earlier at point-blank range. How could he be alive, Mili wondered? She unbuttoned his shirt to look for the bullet wound, but instead discovered that his chest was protected by a very thick vest made of some dense fabric. Whatever it was, it had saved Trump's life.

Mili called an operator on her mobile phone and told her to send whatever paramedics and ambulances were available from New Babylon's hospital. Four Trump vigilantes who had taken shots were dead. The remaining man with a bullet in his abdomen was still alive. Mili had no first-aid supplies of any kind, but used wads of cloth torn from her sleeves to stuff the man's hemorrhaging wound.

The park filled rapidly with Sekhmet streetwalkers. Trump sat up. Then he stood and checked each of the fallen men.

"I'm glad you're alive," Mili told him.

"Only because I'm wearing a bulletproof vest," he replied.

Trump gazed at the route the killer had used to escape.

"I can't believe that son of a bitch is gone," he cried frustrated. "I shot him from no more than three feet away."

"Do you believe it was Jack?" Mili asked.

"I don't know," Trump answered. "I didn't get a clear view of his face. But who else could it have been if not him?"

"I think it *was* Jack," Mili said. "Flaunting his presence. When we take him down, I'm going to stick my finger in the hole your bullet made."

Two ambulances arrived. One departed immediately with the sole surviving vigilante. Sirens wailing, it screeched down the streets hoping its errand of mercy would not be in vain. The rest of Trump's men had their bodies bundled in blankets and loaded into the remaining ambulance.

Several blocks away the man who had called himself Proxmire, and Fulbright, and many other stolen names, sat on a metal kitchen chair in his apartment. He had cleaned and sterilized his bullet wound, packed it with bandage waddings, and given himself a shot of penicillin. The slug was still lodged somewhere inside of his shoulder. But wherever it was it hadn't killed him. Yet.

It might cause a septic infection. It could migrate. Or he might get really lucky and just shit it out. He had taken his Colt revolvers to the square tonight because a demon had tipped him off to Trump's plan. No one on Earth had caught him when he was alive. What made anyone in Hell think that it would be different now? He'd take time to recover and then show them what happened when Jack the Ripper went looking for revenge.

He leaned back in the chair and dabbed a piece of gauze at the blood and lymph leaking from the bullet hole. His flesh ached agonizingly around the wound. He wondered if it had hurt the Sekhmets this much when he had slit their throats. He hoped so. He hoped it hurt a hundred times worse. Maybe next time he'd cut off their faces and rip open their bellies *before* he killed them. Yes, that's exactly what he'd do.

But first he was going to track down Trump. He'd actually shot that arrogant piece of shite first, but somehow Trump had survived and had managed to shoot him back. What the Hell? The man rested his head against the back of his chair and stopped thinking. He felt himself passing out. That was all right. There would be other nights. Always had been. Always would be.

CHAPTER THIRTEEN

Mili was sitting at Mardie's kitchen table, drinking sweet sherry. She was miserable over last night's fiasco. And she was sure that the man on the bench had indeed been Jack the Ripper, baiting all of Hell to confront him. Everything about the failed operation bothered her. He had sat for hours smoking on the park bench. Had managed to come to the square with a workman's satchel carrying two American revolvers and God knew how much ammunition. Had successfully taken down Trump and killed four of his vigilantes. And to top it all off, no one—including her—had gotten a clear of his face.

She'd called Lucifer and talked about the whole disastrous episode. He was, of course, familiar with Trump's secret organization and told her that it would be a routine request to replace the slain vigilantes' Hellion bodies. Not that he would look forward to appearing before Jehovah to make that request. Heavenly bodies for the saints and Hellion bodies for the damned were exclusively created in Paradise. And only with God's permission. Satan had quizzed Mili on whether Trump had revealed anything about himself when discussing the existence of his group of armed sentinels.

"You mean his stories about being bullied on the World War II gunship?" Mili asked.

"That for sure. Anything else?"

"Only that he was Dorian Gray," Mili said getting irritated. "Why did you keep *that* from me?"

"What would have been the point of telling you?" Satan replied defensively.

"You also didn't think that I needed to be informed about Trump's covert organization!"

"They're not really covert," the Devil argued. "They're more like Justices of the Peace. They function as conservators of public civility, if you will, rather than as police or detectives."

"By torturing people?" Mili countered.

"They only deal with evil-doers."

"And after they die?"

"I petition God for a replacement Hellion body."

"And he grants them?" Mili was incredulous.

"Routinely. He rather likes it when a terrible man or woman gets exactly what they have coming to them."

"I am horrified."

"Truly? You have never wished that a serial killer, or a wife murderer, or even a wicked dictator could be punished more severely than the inconvenience and discomfort of damnation?"

"I always thought that going to Hell *was* their punishment."

"Hell is easy street compared to the likes of what Joseph Stalin, Mao Zedong, or even Jeffrey Dahmer deserve. So, I recruited Trump to help me make sure that if any of those monsters so much as lifts a finger to resume their evil ways down here they will receive the punishment they deserve."

"I am speechless," Mili declared.

"Well, it's who I am," Lucifer answered sounding offended. "And it's what I do."

Mili was still recovering from that blunt and awful conversation hours later. How could her husband not only allow, but *condone* such terror in the underworld? When she shared bits of their conversation with Mardie, her sister had reacted very positively about the Devil's team of avengers. And when Mili disagreed, telling her that *she* found it repugnant, Mardie had looked her straight in the eye and asked her how she thought the six million Jews who'd been starved, beaten, and gassed by the Nazi's would feel about it? Mili stared at her. Then she got it. There was no more conversation about Trump's secret charter. Then or ever.

※ ※ ※

Mardie rose from her chair and reached into a kitchen cupboard. She spoke to Mili as she did.

"I've been saving a special treat for you, and I think you should have it now. It's a bit time consuming to prepare, but we have all day to figure out what to do after getting our asses kicked by Jack."

Mardie pulled out her fondue pot and showed it to Mili. Her sister was so delighted she clapped her hands.

"Cake balls dipped in chocolate!" Mili cried.

"Yes!" Mardie yelped and set the fondue pot, a handful of dipping forks, and a small butane burner on the table. She laid out table settings for Mili and herself while she explained.

"Cake balls hadn't shown up in the regular food shipments from Heaven forever," she explained. "So, I asked Trump to tell Lucifer that I wanted some. He asked *when* did I want them, and I said lickety-split. Anyway, two boxes got here today." She reached into another cupboard and pulled out a large package of cake balls. She also fetched several Toblerone chocolate bars and sat down to get the dipping sauce going. She unwrapped the bars, broke them into pieces, and put them in the pot. She added cream, lit the burner, and put the pot on.

"This is so wonderful of you, Mardie," Mili said.

"Better than tea," her twin answered. "Even better than booze! And speaking of drinks, do you want ice water or milk?"

"Would both be all right?" Mili asked.

"Both would be perfect!" Mardie told her.

Mardie went to the ice box for bottled water, whole milk, and ice cubes. As she filled the glasses, she asked Mili the question of the hour.

"So, what's next with Mad Jack?"

"First off," Mili answered, "I'm going to dig out whichever wanker gave us away to the Ripper. And I'm pretty sure it has to be someone in Lucifer's office."

Mardie frowned.

"A mole?"

"Jack wouldn't have brought two Colt six-shooters to a park unless he'd been told there was going to be a slaughter."

"Couldn't the spy just as easily have been among Trump's vigilantes?"

"If he was, he got shot for his trouble. But I think it more likely that the spy is someone tucked deep inside *Lucifer's* organization. They will go quiet until Jack resurfaces. And that may be awhile. The Ripper was wounded, perhaps very seriously, by Trump. He won't be working the rape-and-murder circuit for a while. When and if he comes back, we'll put the Sekhmet ladies of the night back on the street along with their Shapeshifter back-ups."

Mardie opened the box of cakes and filled Mili's plate. She took a few for herself as well, then stirred the melting chocolate and nodded at Mili. Her twin knew the cake ball playbook by heart and put three of them on her prong and dipped them into the melted chocolate.

"So, what about a plan B?" Mardie suggested. "Doesn't simply repeating the stakeout put the Sekhmets at even more risk with the Ripper intent on revenge?"

"Posing the Sekhmets to bring Jack out actually was plan A, darling," Mili told her. "Plan B was Trump's plan. Bring along the vigilantes. And that wound up getting the shit shot out of everybody."

"Well, trying plan A at this point is just going to get the Sekhmets' throats cut," Mardie countered.

Mili shook her head. She raised her prong of chocolate-covered cake balls to check on progress, then dipped it in the chocolate again.

"Every Sekhmet prostitute will have a Shapeshifter close by watching her," she reminded Mardie, "armed and ready to intervene in an instant."

Mili lifted up her cake balls again and checked again. She re-dipped them.

"Are you a two or a three dipper?" Mardie asked.

"Three dipper," she said. "This is the third dunk for these. Three times builds enough chocolate to truly complement the cake."

Mardie gazed at her sister and her face became pensive.

"I never understood why Mum liked candy more than me," she said sadly.

This topic was a tender one, and had not been broached for years. The twins' mother had had a sugar fascination that led to an addiction to sweets that occupied her desires, her activities, and her dreams. She was obviously substituting treats for the things in life that she had not received as a child or as a bride.

"Mother loved you, Mardie," Mili said to her sister. "But she could not relate to you. Your outrageous behaviors and desperate cries for love were frightening to her. She felt safe around me only because I became a total sugar addict to keep her from pushing me away, too."

"Did you know you were doing that when you were little?" Mardie asked.

Mili shook her head.

"No. Only later. But when we were children and you fussed out of frustration, it put me in that much stronger of a position to be needed by Mother. I never reached out to you, fearing that you'd somehow jinx my grip on Mum's affection." Mili looked miserable.

Mardie took her sister's hand.

"Thank you for sharing. I can't believe how lucky we are to be together *now*, even if it is in Hell."

"I'm just grateful that we're women," Mili responded. "Can you imagine two men holding hands and sharing their feelings like this?"

"Ha!" Mardie snorted.

"I love you," Mili told her.

"And I love you."

Mili squeezed Mardie's hand and gently pulled away.

"Sorry," she muttered and nodded at the fondue pot. "Cake balls."

* * *

Mardie walked to the Hells Bells supermarket near her house. She had sufficient cake balls and plenty of chocolate for Mili's treat, but she needed to buy some more burners for the fondue pot. It was bloody hot out, of course, and as she walked Mardie watched her every step on the broken and ruined sidewalk.

Folks were out, sans tops or bottoms, just wearing thongs for minimal coverage and maximum exposure. Some were walking. Some were riding bicycles. Mardie bucked the fashionistas and wore white shorts and a pink tank top with a *Stephen Universe* cartoon on the front. She loved that show. Everyone could be anything they wanted to be. Wouldn't that have been grand back on Earth?

She walked into the supermarket and was very surprised to find that it was air conditioned. Nicely air conditioned. *Fully* air conditioned. What the—? The store had never been air conditioned before. On her way to the cooking supplies aisle, she passed the produce section. Fruits and vegetables were displayed in abundance and shoppers were clearly amazed and happy.

There was a clerk spraying down the lettuce and cucumbers. He was a forty-something Hellion with a handsome face and a nice build. He had on a white short sleeve shirt, white work pants, and a blue apron with a bib. Mardie walked up to him.

"G'day, gorgeous," he greeted her in a heavy Australian accent. "Busy tonight?"

Mardie was pleasantly surprised to have the hunk flirt with her.

"Thank you, I am," she said. "Can you tell me when the fruits and vegetables became so fresh and plentiful?"

"Just like me, doll, fresh and plentiful."

Mardie grinned.

"You got the fresh part down for sure," she said.

"Do you want to check out the plentiful?" he asked.

"Only in my imagination, good looking. So, what's going on here?"

"The Ben-Yehuda Kibbutz has the contract for fresh produce now. They insisted that air conditioning be installed in every Hells Bells' outlet that carries their citrus, berries, melons, tropical fruits, and vegetables." The clerk stepped closer. "How about a drink tonight?"

"When did all this happen? I don't come in here often."

"About a month ago. How about a drink *tomorrow* night?"

Mardie was on the verge of saying yes—despite her relationship with Bowles—but she was
saved from temptation when she spotted none other than Albert Einstein walking toward the
tobacco aisle. She turned and followed him.

The clerk called after her.

"Wednesday night? Thursday night? This weekend?"

Mardie waved over her shoulder. Annoying piece of shite, she thought. Although she'd take his approach over that of Jack the Ripper. She reached out and tapped Professor Einstein on the shoulder. He turned and smiled.

"Hello, Mardie. I haven't seen you in years."

The famous physicist was wearing his favorite green wool sweater, brown corduroy pants, and old brown shoes. His hair floated like a white cloud above his brow, but it was washed and carefully primped. Did he use a blow dryer on that effervescent mop?

"Actually, Dr. Einstein, I saw you at the Good News Club just a couple of nights ago. Lucifer and my sister Mili were there, too. We all had a drink together."

Einstein looked confused, but then he smiled and nodded.

"You're absolutely right!" he said cheerfully. "You were waiting to see *Einstein in Jerusalem.*"

Mardie laughed out loud.

"Yes," she played along. "But you left before it started."

"Been there. Done that," the professor declared.

Mardie laughed again. Oh, my, she thought.

"Are you headed for the tobacco section, Dr. Einstein?" she asked.

"Yes, I am. I need a tin of pipe tobacco and some cigarettes. Maybe you could help me. The tobacco I am looking for is called Whiff of the Sea. It gives off the smell of tuna. Always reminds me of the ocean."

Mardie frowned. As far as she knew, Einstein hadn't grown up *or* lived by the sea ever. What did he know about how tuna smelled? Besides, fresh tuna didn't smell like tuna. Only *canned* tuna smelled like tuna. That, and apparently Einstein's favorite tobacco blend. She looked at the cans on the shelves while the professor searched the cigarette section. He reached for a box of unfiltered Pall Malls. She recognized that as the brand Hugh Everett III chain-smoked.

Before she could ask if the smokes were for Hugh, Dr. Einstein put the Pall Malls back and pulled out a box of Gauloises Red. Unfiltered French cigarettes. Mardie knew that iconic brand. She had smoked Reds during endless London nights when her favorite bars and pubs had reserved chairs for her ever-present fanny. She was sure that she still had scars on her lungs from smoking them.

"Dr. Einstein?" she asked

He looked her way.

"If you are purchasing cigarettes for Hugh Everett, you need to buy the Pall Malls."

"Thank you, Mardie," the professor answered. "Did you find Whiff of the Sea?"

Mardie pulled a can off the shelf and showed the label to Einstein.

"That's the one," he said.

"Do you want more than one can?"

"Whatever for?" he asked.

Mardie handed the can to him and refrained from commenting.

"Please tell Hugh hello from me."

Einstein squinted at her through his rimless glasses.

"Why would I do that?"

"Because I remember him with affection."

"I do, too. That's why I look forward to his visits so much. We talk a lot about wormholes. That is *my* theory, you know. In 1935 my colleague Nathan Rose and I were the first scientists to theorize their existence and describe them as bridges connecting different layers of space and time."

"Is Everett visiting you now?" Mardie asked.

"No, that's why I can't tell him hello for you."

"But you're buying him cigarettes."

"Yes. He's coming tomorrow."

"Then tell him hello from me then."

Einstein frowned.

"Mardie, I like you," he told her. "But you're pushy."

CHAPTER FOURTEEN

Mardie walked back home thinking about Einstein's bridges. Son of a bitch. He and his colleague had proposed the very first wormholes theory in 1935. They were figuring out how the physics of space worked decades ahead of anyone else on the planet.

Mardie stopped and watched a crew of street workers filling holes in the road. Several other pedestrians had stopped to watch as well. Mardie had *never* seen anyone work on *any* street in Hell. The arterials were barely traversable and then only by half-mad cab drivers or constitutionally fearless individuals like Paul Pfotenhauer.

A lot of men dressed in green work shirts and pants were working on the street, shoveling new asphalt onto the damaged surfaces. Behind them were huge machines laying down black gooey stuff on top of the road after the repairs. Other machines behind those rolled it smooth. Mardie looked at the logo on the door of one of them. *BYK Enterprises* was stenciled on it with a Star of David on top.

Well, I'll be damned, Mardie thought. The repairs were being done by David Ben-Gurion's kibbutz. It had repaired the freeways and now they were working on city streets. If she had any money, she'd be buying up properties for gas stations and car dealerships. Decent roads was about to change the way everything worked in New Babylon. New streets would encourage new cars, and it had to be only a matter of time before Lucifer would contract with the kibbutz to spruce up New Babylon and clean its filthy skyscrapers. They would be sparkling towers of steel and glass. Gonna be the effin' Los Angeles of Hell.

Mardie walked on watching her every step. The kibbutz apparently hadn't bid for a contract to work on the sidewalks yet. Watching for hazards Mardie thought again about what Einstein had said regarding wormholes. *They were bridges connecting different layers of space and time.* In an instant she realized that the universe had handed her a plum. Taking her life in her hands she ran the rest of the way home. She excitedly told Mili about what Einstein had said. Mili immediately called Pfotenhauer and asked him to fetch them to the kibbutz. She and Mardie needed see Lucifer as soon as possible.

✳ ✳ ✳

Pfotenhauer picked up the Wickett sisters just minutes after Mili had called him. He, in turn, called Lucifer just before they arrived at the kibbutz. The Devil was waiting with both children when the car arrived. Sriracha was holding his dad's hand. Little Mardie was standing next to a boy from the kibbutz holding *his* hand. Mili ran to Lucifer's arms. After a hug and a very nice kiss, she reached down and picked up Sriracha. He smiled at her and said shalom.

Mili laughed happily, hugged him hard, and then turned and looked at Little Mardie.

"Mother, this is Arie Millatiner," she said. "He lives here on the kibbutz."

Arie bowed and said, "Pleased to meet you."

Mili smiled and nodded.

Arie was a handsome boy with curly brown hair and amber eyes. He was wearing black workpants and a white short sleeve shirt. Little Mardie had on a yellow work dress and brown boots.

"Love your outfit, honey," Mili told her.

Little Mardie grinned.

"I'm helping in the apple orchards now. That's where I met Arie."

"An early harvest," Mili said sweetly.

She looked down at Sriracha in her arms, and he looked back.

"Is this the part," he asked quite seriously, "where you ask me if I set any fires lately?"

"I *never* ask you that, son."

"Well, you should today," he responded.

Mili arched an eyebrow. Then she complied.

"Sriracha, did you start any fires today?"

"I did not, Mother. I was in Hebrew school."

"Goodness! Was it fun?"

"Yes, it was. We did crafts and cooking, and sang songs about the letters in the Hebrew Aleph-bet. You know, the *alphabet*? I also learned how to say please and thank you. Thank you is toda. Please is burtbacharach."

Mili gazed at her son.

"You are so smart. You learned both of those at school?"

"I learned toda there. Daddy taught me the other one."

Mili shot Lucifer a glance. He popped up his eyebrows as though to say *me*?

Mardie got a round of hugs from everyone, and Mili introduced her and Pfot to her Little Mardie's new squeeze. Actually, her *first ever* squeeze. Arie responded politely and respectfully. Little Mardie seemed happier than her mother had seen her in a long time. Mili felt old and out of it gazing at her daughter. Why hadn't she realized what her fifteen-year-old girl needed? *Arie* was what Little Mardie needed. Yes, the times they were a-changin'.

"The dining hall is open," Lucifer announced. "Everyone ready for dinner?"

"Will the food be different than the last two nights?" Sriracha asked.

"Actually, yes," the Devil told his son. "Your uncle Moshe spoke to one of the cooks who's from America, and some new things will be served. Grilled cheese sandwiches, Aleph-bet soup with letters made of noodles, and pizza."

"Hooray!" Little Mardie shouted. Everyone was startled and stared at her. She blushed and spoke to Sriracha. "I think you were the one who was supposed to say that."

"Hooray!" Sriracha cried and clapped his hands. "I never had pizza before! What is it?"

Everyone walked through the buffet line together and then went separate directions. Satan accompanied David Ben-Gurion. Pfot dined with four elderly ladies whom he had recently met. Little Mardie and Arie joined a big batch of young people. Moshe Dayan asked for cuts in line from Mardie and together they decided to find a place outside to eat and talk.

It was all fine with Mili, who sat with Sriracha and watched him eat his first slice of pepperoni pizza. He rolled it up and stuck it in his mouth like a cigar. Mili laughed so hard she spilled her glass of red wine on her white shorts. It didn't matter. She was thrilled that Sriracha wasn't lighting up his pizza cigar and smoking it.

After dinner, Siracha ran off with of a slew of kids to watch Barney the Dinosaur videos. Their parents assured Mili that Sriracha would be brought to their guest apartment after the kids had seen their shows. Mili wondered if the programs were in Hebrew. She didn't know about the kibbutz kids, but she knew that *she'd* enjoy Barney a lot more that way. Toda! Burtbacharach!

Mardie walked with Mili and Lucifer back to the guest apartment. She plunked down on an overstuffed chair. Mili sat down on the sofa next to Lucifer only to have him jump back up and head for the kitchen.

"I've got a surprise for you ladies," he called, and returned with a bottle of Rusack Chardonnay. He showed the label to both Mili and Mardie. "One of the first bottles of white wine ever produced on Catalina Island."

Mili remembered that Cleopatra once had a monopoly on white wine distribution in Hell. And she specifically recalled how the Egyptian temptress had *earned* that most favored position from the Devil. She felt a sting of jealousy, but then remembered that the entrepreneurial sexpot had to settle for Antony while she wound up with Lucifer. Mili smiled as her handsome husband set wine glasses for everyone. He opened the wine and poured.

"To love," Satan said raising his glass.

"And marriage," Mili added.

"Hear, hear!" Mardie said, and they all drank.

"So, what brought the two lovely Wickett sisters to the kibbutz for this get together?" Lucifer asked. "An attempt to resolve the riddle of who messed with *Abraham Sacrifices Isaac*?"

"Ha! You big phony!" Mili declared. "We found out from an unimpeachable source that *you* did it."

Satan smiled mischievously.

"Guilty as charged," he confessed. "It was a lot tougher to pull off than you can possibly imagine. The Evangelicals who put on these plays have ironclad principles."

"Yet you did manage to talk them into doing it, didn't you?" Mili asked.

"Yes, but I didn't really care about that old story. The one I was trying to get them to do was *Jesus Didn't Rise from the Dead*."

Mili and Mardie just stared at Lucifer.

"Grow up," Mili finally said. "You might as well have tried to stage *God Doesn't Exist*."

The Devil smiled and wagged a finger at his wife.

"Couldn't do that one," he said. "Bill Nye already owns the copyright."

"We came to the kibbutz to talk about something serious, Lu," Mili said.

"More important than God's existence?" Lucifer grinned naughtily. "OK, fine. I'm done." He topped off the ladies' wine glasses.

"Hugh Everett has been visiting Albert Einstein," Mili said.

"He sure has," Satan acknowledged. "For years now. I know that you and Mardie don't have much respect for the demons down here, but they are the best spies anywhere."

"I'll have to take your word for that, dear," Mili said. "And speaking of which, a matter pertaining to them and your other staff members needs to be broached sooner or later."

Lucifer's face got serious.

"Now?"

"Later. Right now, I want to talk about Einstein and Everett. Mardie ran into Dr. Einstein at the supermarket today buying cigarettes for Hugh. He told her that Everett is coming to visit him tomorrow night. Mardie and I want to be there."

"I do?" Mardie piped up surprised.

"Yes. You were the one who told me about Albert Einstein's time bridges."

"Are we talking about wormholes?" Lucifer asked.

"Yes," Mardie answered. "Einstein theorized that there are bridges, aka wormholes, that not only connect *places* in the universe, but also bond *different eras and historical events.*"

"You mean time travel," Satan said.

"Precisely." Mili interrupted. "I want Albert Einstein and Hugh Everett to find a wormhole to England in the autumn of the year 1888. Mardie and I are going to go back and find Jack the Ripper."

Lucifer looked anxious.

"I am aware of Dr. Einstein's theories. Aren't you afraid of changing history?" he asked. "Jehovah's not a big fan of that."

"This from the guy who wants to stage *God Doesn't Exist*?" Mili asked.

"That's just a play, darling. But *you* actually want to go back to 1888 and find the real Jack the Ripper."

"Damn straight."

Lucifer shook his head.

Mardie jumped in.

"We aren't going to change anything, Lu. We'll find out Jack's identity by showing up at the exact spot where he intends to commit a murder. We'll note his features and build, and then we'll come back and track the asshole down right here in Hell."

"That could work," Satan conceded.

"It's the *only* thing that will work," Mili emphasized. She high-fived Mardie. "Well said!"

Mardie grinned.

"Sisters, remember?"

✳ ✳ ✳

Late that night, Lucifer was spooning Mili's naked body and whispered in her ear, "Feel like messing around?"

"I don't know, love," she answered. "Every time we stay over at the kibbutz, I get pregnant."

"Well, that's true, I guess. Like the Bible says though, it's good for a man to have his quiver full of arrows."

"Yeah, right. You personally like the part where you put *your* arrow in *my* quiver."

The Devil pulled Mili close and kissed her neck. "Also, Mardie thinks that I've already been showing signs of being pregnant. Moody, tired, cranky. Wanting salt and sugar in excess."

"And the verdict?"

"She bought me a couple of pregnancy kits at Hells Bells when she ran into Dr. Einstein. You're going to be a father again."

"I'm thrilled, darling!" Satan said and rolled Mili onto her back. "And to tell you the truth, I could already tell that you were pregnant."

"You do realize that it's *this* activity that's resulting in babies?" Mili teased.

"Of course, I do," Lucifer whispered back. "Let's go for twins!"

CHAPTER FIFTEEN

"Of course, it's possible," Albert Einstein answered Mili. "You can travel backward *and* forward in time. It's locating the right bridges that's the challenge. There are probably trillions of bridges throughout the universe. But finding them and discovering where they lead appears to be a totally hit-or-miss proposition. Here's a bridge to Xian on March 21, 1267. There's a bridge to Florence on May 6, 1648. Want to go to Armor, South Dakota, on September 1, 1926? Time bridges are everywhere and they go to *every* date and time. But as I just said, finding a bridge that will take you to the exact time and place you want is nigh on impossible."

"But not *completely* impossible," Hugh Everett III interjected. He was thin and handsome, bearded and tan, wearing jeans and a long-sleeve plaid work shirt. He actually owned a small farm on his alternate home world, so he wasn't just dressed like a rancher wannabee. Everett still smoked, and during the evening he worked his way through three packs of the Gauloises cigarettes that Einstein had given him, as well as several Crown Royal Perfect Manhattans.

Dr. Einstein had been quite happy when the Wickett sisters showed up unannounced and proceeded to ask him and Everett endless questions about finding and using time bridges. It grew late and Mardie had gone out and brought back soup and sandwiches from Hells Bells.

"Not impossible," Everett repeated. "At first glance, there does appear to be a randomness in the placement of wormholes, but for the last couple of years, I have worked out a set of algorithms designed to take into consideration variables like the distance between two places, the size of the gap in time, the probable path between them in folded space, the locations of particular bridges whose destinations have been identified, and for that matter, bridges that Lucifer's fallen angels tell me exist. Hundreds additional factors are applied as well, all utilized toward realizing the singular goal of mapping out a likely place where a person could pinpoint the wormhole that would take them to an *exact* historical place and time."

"Goodness," Mardie said.

Albert nodded.

"Are there moments in time that *you* want to visit, Hugh?" Mili asked.

"No, none," Hugh answered and lit up a fresh cigarette. "I'd enjoy working on *your* request with Dr. Einstein, however. It's a monumental challenge. But how often does the opportunity present itself to partner with the greatest scientist who ever lived?"

"I wouldn't mind having some pretty women join us," Einstein added.

Everyone ignored him.

Hugh went on.

"I think I could design some metrics and establish predictive analytics that would narrow down the algorithmic results as to where you'd have to go in the universe to find a bridge to August, 1888. When Jack the Ripper first appeared on the scene."

"How long would that take?" Mili asked.

"If I work with the existing computers on my world, I would guess three or four years."

Mili sat back in her chair and drank down her wine. Three or four years? She felt herself sinking into an instant funk.

"On the other hand," Everett went on, "if your husband can get me access to one of IBM's artificial intelligence Watson super computers—by far the smartest and fastest computer around—I could probably narrow down the location of such a bridge within a few days. Maybe even in only a few hours."

Mardie looked stunned.

Mili slowly shook her head.

"As connected as Lucifer is," she responded, "I don't think he's got the pull to get IBM to lend one out."

"Does he have the pull to just steal one?" Hugh asked.

Mili thought of the state-of-the-art genetics lab that Satan had procured for her. Overnight.

"*That* I think he can do," she answered.

"So how do we get him involved?"

"I'll talk to him tonight. We're staying at the kibbutz, and he loves to hang out late with David Ben-Gurion and Moshe Dayan and just schmooze."

"So, you'll ask him then?"

Mili shook her head.

"He always feels especially romantic when he's far away from the cares of the city," she added.

"She'll ask him *then*," Mardie explained.

Mili smiled.

"Where do you want it delivered, Hugh?" she asked.

"Anywhere. The first Watson filled up a whole room. The current Watson is only the size of a pizza box."

Einstein jumped to his feet excited.

"Can he get two?"

✳ ✳ ✳

Early the next morning Mili woke to find Lucifer gone from their bed. She rose, looked for a note or a text explaining his absence, but found nothing. She peeked at the children in the spare bedrooms. Both kids were asleep. Good. It was only eight in the morning, so they'd probably sleep hours more. She made herself a pot of coffee and then showered. She called Mardie who was staying in one of the dormitories, but got her voicemail. She fixed herself some coffee and waited.

At six minutes after nine o'clock, Lucifer walked in. He was carrying three large square white boxes, each about two inches thick. The Devil put them on the kitchen table where Mili was sitting and gave her a gentle kiss. He said hello and poured himself a cup of coffee. He sat down and nodded at the boxes.

"Watsons?" Mili guessed.

Satan's face lit up, quite pleased with his success.

"Just like you asked for last night," he answered.

"How did you manage to steal three?" Mili questioned.

"*Please*," Lucifer replied. "These are not stolen."

"Well, I know you didn't buy them."

"You *can't* buy them, girlfriend."

"Okay. So how did you achieve this feat?"

The Devil took a drink of his coffee and grinned.

"While it is true that IBM won't sell Watsons to the public yet, it has placed a number of them on a trial basis with the United States military. I made some calls to a few high-ranking friends, and voila, three Watsons have been generously *loaned* to yours truly."

"I am impressed."

"Yes." Lucifer allowed himself a self-satisfied smirk. "And you thought buying souls was so passé."

Mili rolled her eyes.

"So, who do these go to?" she asked. "Einstein, Everett, and who else?"

"*You*, my talented wife. Enjoy."

Mili gave her spouse a sweet smile.

"You are truly my wonderful provider."

"Me and my captive souls."

* * *

Pfotenhauer dropped Mili at Mardie back at Mardie's house in New Babylon after she'd made a stop at Albert Einstein's house to drop off two Watsons for him and Hugh Everett. Hugh was not there, but Dr. Einstein said he expected him back again that night. The plan was for him to team up with Einstein for as long as it took to locate the time bridge Mili and Mardie needed to travel to London in August, 1888.

Mili left her Watson at the kibbutz, happy with Lucifer's gesture. However, none of her tasks required its trillion operation-points at 10 to the 12th power speed per second. Her iPad suited virtually all of her online needs, and if the rare occasion should arise when it did not, she could always power up her portable Mac. Its memory and speed matched the human brain, which was good enough for her.

She wondered what kind of brain Lucifer possessed as an archangel, and then dared to imagine what kind of intelligence Jehovah must possess. Would the day come years from now when Watson challenged the Devil or God to a game of *Jeopardy*? It would make for mind-boggling TV. And even more entertaining than watching Fox News, which actually she refused to do. Sometimes Mardie did and laughed her ass off.

Mili sat and drank Cava at Mardie's house, a sparkling wine from Spain. It was quite similar to her favorite French champagne, Dom Perignon. It was yeasty with tiny bubbles, but about a thousand percent cheaper. She was searching the internet for images of period British costumes worn by women in the late 1880s. Mardie was drinking chardonnay and looking up the same thing using the Mac portable.

"Remember Mardie," Mili said when they started, "you are not searching for clothes that *you* would have worn in 1888. We are searching for clothing that *regular* women wore."

Mardie gazed at Mili as if waiting for a clarification.

Mili explained.

"You always dress in clothes that look as though you're waiting for some nice-looking man to help you take them off. In late nineteenth century London you will need to wear something less suggestive."

Mardie frowned. She understood, but didn't like being lectured.

"And what will women of the night be wearing to signal *their* availability to such as Jack the Ripper?"

Mili shook her head.

"I'll find out," she said. "But I want *us* to blend in. *Not* draw the Ripper's attention."

"But maybe we *should* draw his attention," Mardie insisted. "Nothing like staring Jack down face-to-face, so we will recognize him back here afterwards."

"No," Mili disagreed. "We don't want face-to-face. That wicked man could slice both of our throats open before we could even cry out."

"I thought he raped his victims before killing them."

"Not always."

"Oh."

"Yes."

Mardie found pictures of women's dresses that had been fashionable in 1888 London. They were long elegant gowns with bustles underneath—mesh frames fastened to the waist—that made female asses ride high and look sassy. In addition, such dresses also required a corset, a vest-like garment wrapped around the torso with strings in the back that pulled tight to shrink the waist while simultaneously thrusting up the wearer's bosoms. If this was *normal* women's clothing, Mardie thought, what the Hell had the prostitutes worn?

It turned out hookers favored clothing that was actually more modest, but a whole lot more versatile. Young streetwalkers wore blouses with elastic hems at the top and no brassieres, making a pull-down display of wares a snap. Skirts were long, worn without underwear, and required only a quick yank to expose the naked pleasures inside. The article accompanying the images explained that men would often take their pleasure right where the whores solicited them. Leaning against a building wall or bending over doggie style. Goodness. Mardie kept looking.

"Find anything?" Mili asked after a while.

"I discovered one outfit that I wouldn't mind wearing."

"Show me."

Mardie turned the screen towards Mili. Her twin smiled and nodded.

"Very cool and very practical. Jacket and pants. Years ahead of its time. Not until Coco Channel took Paris by storm decades later did that kind of casual wear become the rage for women. Along with sun tans, cigarettes, and love affairs."

"*That's* what I'm going to wear," Mardie decided.

"Ask me if I'm surprised," Mili told her.

"You have to admit that it looks comfortable."

"It *looks* like you want to get fucked."

"I don't mind that look," Mardie said.

"Of course, you don't," Mili snapped. "But what if Jack is the one who comes calling?"

"You'll save me."

Mili shook her head.

"And if it's not the Ripper?" she asked Mardie.

"Then I'll fuck the one I'm with."

Mili shook her head.

"Keep looking," she told her twin.

The sisters viewed a lot of outfits. Mili brewed up a pot of coffee and drank cup after cup. Mardie continued to drink wine and turned mellow and happy. Mili became caffeinated to the point where any smart remark from Mardie would likely have gotten her whacked with the coffee pot. It didn't get to that though as Mardie grew more and more sweetly gregarious, obliviating the need for Mili to bean her.

In the end, both sisters picked ordinary middle-class dresses with modestly-sized bustles and corsets. Mili refused to wear high heels in case they needed to flee. Which was fine with Mardie, but she insisted that *she* would be wearing them. Be it Jack she met—or just some jack-off—she was staying put wherever she stood.

"So, what now?" Mardie asked.

"I'll send images and sizes to Lucifer and ask him to have his folks provide the costumes."

"You have a husband who spoils you," Mardie commented.

"Yes, I do. And I am so grateful."

"Did he find out yet that you're three months along?"

"He knew before I did. His demon spies told him."

"How did *they* find out?" Mardie asked.

"Hell if I know."

"That makes me feel weird."

"Doesn't it, though?" Mili agreed.

"Maybe the demons have x-ray eyes or something," Mardie suggested. "They are, after all, fallen angels and may possess talents that we don't even know about."

"You mean like playing harps?" Mili suggested.

"I distinctly said talents that we *don't* know about."

"Heh, heh."

Mardie eyed her sister.

"Did you do that on purpose?"

Mili grinned a smart-ass grin.

"Why don't you ask my Watson?"

"You left it at the kibbutz," Mardie told her. Then she panicked. "What if Sriracha gets his hands on it?" she cried, instantly worried.

"Can you imagine the things he could look up? How to cook hotdogs. The distance to the nearest candy store. What to do if you set your bed on fire."

"Very funny," Mili replied. "He's only five. He doesn't read or write. And he can't use a keyboard."

"He doesn't have to," Mardie shot back. "All he has to do is *talk* to Watson and it will do whatever he asks."

"Son of a bitch!" Mili shouted.

CHAPTER SIXTEEN

Mili stayed over at Mardie's house again. Pfotenhauer called her and asked for permission to head back to the kibbutz. He explained that a friendly widow whom he had gotten to know had invited him to visit, and he wanted to leave early enough to be there for her eight-thirty bedtime. Mili was happy for him, though how and where Pfot and his belle would consummate their mutual attraction was a puzzle to her. The widow slept in a two-story dormitory housed with twenty-four other single women.

Maybe they would just go to sleep together and wake up in the middle of the night to do it. Whenever they made it happen, it wouldn't have the same consequences as her lovemaking with Lucifer did. She patted her small belly. Number three was indeed on the way. She wondered if it was a boy or a girl? Whoever would be joining the family, Mili was determined that he or she would not be named Tapatio or Cholula, Tabasco or Worchester.

Mili and Mardie stayed up late talking and eating cake balls. Mardie asked her twin to share some stories about her favorite adventures, and Mili did, quite pleased that Mardie had asked. She related cases about a murdered billionaire. (Done in by his wife.) An assassinated parliament member. (Offed by his own party.) A butchered engineering genius. (Retired by one of his employer's robots.) A poisoned mistress. (Kissed goodbye by her lover's spouse.) And even a terminated bishop. (Sent to Heaven by the organist who'd had it with his Sunday hymn selections.) Scotland Yard had always assigned Mili the most puzzling cases, and nary a one had she failed to solve.

Mardie enjoyed the tales of Mili's successes. She had a question, however, and asked about any assignments that had required off-the-record activities in order to be satisfactorily concluded.

"Any instances where *you* levied justice on a perpetrator yourself?" she asked straight out.

Mili stared at Mardie for a long time. That was a question no one had ever asked her before. Not Yard officials. Not colleagues. Not police. Not relatives of the deceased. She was sure that other inspectors had solved occasional cases using *personal* options, as Inspector Abberline had confessed to her at the Good News Club, but no one else had ever, ever confessed to such while she had worked at the Yard.

"There was one occasion," Mili answered at last. She gazed at Mardie who sat waiting silently. "The cook at a home for orphans came to the Yard and reported that government stipends to purchase food were, in fact, being pocketed by the managing director while the orphans themselves were being secretly butchered and served as food. The missing children were designated as runaways by the director, and readily replaced by other homeless boys and girls from Social Services waiting lists."

"What made the cook suspicious?" Mardie asked. "Did the meat look or taste different?"

Mili shook her head.

"She routinely received packages of ground round and sausage stuffed with fillers and spices. Could have been made from anything. What alerted her that something wasn't right were the concerns of the orphans themselves. They kept asking if she knew where their absent friends had gone. When it finally dawned on her what heinous scheme the managing director had concocted, she went straight to Scotland Yard and was assigned to me.

"I listened to the woman's concerns and made an appointment to visit the orphanage's director. He was a tall, handsome fellow, given to spending a lot of time grooming. He was dismayed by my blunt questions."

"'Who has accused me?'" he demanded.

"'Someone who believed he was about to be eaten,'" I lied.

"The next day I arranged a secret rendezvous with the cook. She never came to the meeting. I made my own clandestine visit to the orphanage and found that my whistleblower had been replaced. I saw how easily the director could dispose of anyone he chose. And at that point I believed I had but a single recourse available to spare the lives of more defenseless orphans."

"So, you had him chopped up for stew?" Mardie asked hopefully.

"Which would have served him right," Mili replied. "No pun intended. I actually contacted Pfotenhauer—at that time my man on the inside of the London mob—and paid him ten thousand pounds of my own money. Five thousand to hire someone to dispose of the orphanage director, and five thousand to keep for himself as a thank you."

Mardie wasn't shocked by her sister's admission. Probably because her own sense of civic propriety had been dulled somewhat by supporting Trump's cadre of vigilantes in their effort to shoot the Ripper to shit without benefit of due process. Or at least *legal* due process. She didn't know how Trump had figured that the man sitting on the park bench was the guilty guy. But the suspect had shot and killed most of Trump's crew, proving his intuition right, as Pyrrhic as that credit might be.

"You trusted Pfot a lot," Mardie said.

"I did, indeed," Mili responded. "Only had to remind him occasionally that if he betrayed me, I'd shoot him between the eyes."

Mardie's eyebrows flipped up.

"But that wasn't really true," Mili said. "I would never have shot him there."

"Thank God," Mardie said relieved.

"I'd have shot him in the clacker bag."

Mardie's face blanched white.

"Poor Pfot," she groaned.

"Yes," Mili agreed. "Sure glad I never had to do *that*."

※ ※ ※

Mili's mobile phone rang early the next morning. It was Lucifer. She picked up and looked at his image on the screen. The Devil used his iPhone for a selfie pose. It appeared that he was standing in front of the big kibbutz building that housed the cafeteria, the offices, and the library.

"Are you watching, babe?" Lucifer asked.

"Yes."

Satan turned his phone camera towards the parking behind him. It was filled with toys of every description. There were huge piles of stuffed animals, and board games stacked into skyscrapers. There were fleets of toy trucks, cars, and construction equipment, and a mighty plastic mountain fitted with miniature railroad trains running around and around it.

"There's more, darling," Lucifer said and panned his phone camera towards the fields in the distance. Mili could see a *full-size* train, a herd of ponies, a fleet of yellow taxis, a variety of new cars and trucks, a dozen military helicopters—and last and best—an amusement park complete with every ride imaginable. It had a large flag flying from the top of the roller coaster that read *SIX FLAGS OVER HELL*. The Devil turned the camera back on himself looking highly entertained.

"So, dearest," he said. "May I call upon your justly famous detectivising skills to explain what has happened here?"

Mili sighed and replied in a monotone voice.

"Sriracha figured out how to use the Watson."

"Indeed, he did!" his father confirmed. "What was your first clue? The mountain full of trains? The fleet of helicopters? The amusement park?"

"But *how* did he do it?" she cried.

"I asked him that very question. He said that he had been futzing with the Watson and it asked him for a user ID. He told the computer that he was Lucifer Morningstar."

"He used *your* name?" Mili was horrified at Sriracha's audacity.

"Aye. He did. After that, whatever he asked for, Watson relayed the requests to my office and my staff scurried to have everything delivered."

"But you're having all of it returned, right?"

Lucifer looked offended by Mili's question.

"Well, of course. Including the Watson."

"Be sure and have its browser cache and cookies deleted," Mili warned him. "Or one of your generals is going to have a lot of answering to do."

"Got it."

"Also, I don't think there is any such word as detectivising."

"Sure, there is. Sriracha told Watson that's what his 'wife' Mrs. Lucifer did and the AI genius promptly added it to its lexicon."

"Just like that?"

"Yes. I also found it quite instructive to watch Sriracha giving Watson an order. I shot a video of him ordering the amusement park. Let me play it for you."

The video began. Sriracha was sitting on a chair at the kitchen table, and the Watson was placed on the table directly in front of him.

"Hello, Watson," Sriracha said.

"Hello, Mr. Morningstar."

"I want to make an order, Watson."

"What would you like, Mr. Morningstar?"

"I want a roller coaster park."

"A theme park that *features* roller coasters and other rides?" Watson clarified.

"Yes. And I want the rides to be for kids five years old."

"Understood. I will generate a list of required purchases and forward it to Mr. Trump."

"Thank you, Watson."

"Trump knew all about this and didn't even call you?" Mili almost shrieked.

"Sweetheart, Trump's assistants take care of these kinds of things without ever going to him."

"Including a friggin' fleet of attack helicopters?" Mili cried.

"Honey it's just *stuff*. Demons brought what Sriracha asked for. They can take it all back."

"It's still ridiculous," Mili said completely upset.

"Watch the rest of the video," Lucifer told her.

"Is there anything else, Mr. Morningstar?" Watson asked Sriracha.

"Yes. Please bring a diamond bracelet for my mom."

"Your mother?"

"Yes. Her name is Mili."

"I show that Milicent Wickett is your spouse."

"But she's nice as a mom, too. And she is great at detectivising."

"Do you have specifications for the diamond necklace?"

"Lots of big diamonds."

"Embedded in a gold bracelet?"

"That would be good, Watson," Sriracha said gratefully. "I like you."

"Thank you, Mr. Morningstar. I have to inform you that I have never located anything in my cognitive programming that simulates anything like your ability to shop."

"I don't know what that means."

"You are a better shopper than my programmers ever imagined."

Sriracha stood up and snapped off a crisp salute. The video was over.

Mili had tears in her eyes.

"What a dear little sweetheart," she muttered.

"*So*, darling," Lucifer continued. "Budget-wise, we can keep the fleet of military helicopters *or* the diamond bracelet. Do you want to pick?"

"Very funny."

"Not the helicopters?"

Mili couldn't help but grin.

"I don't want a stolen bracelet, either. I want a new one with a shop receipt."

"I'll mention that to Watson," Satan said.

"Better have Sriracha do it. Watson won't have any idea who the Hell *you* are."

"Ha! Outshopped by my own son," the Devil exclaimed. "And while I have you, doll, have you heard what's happening with the other two boys and their Watsons?"

"I haven't heard a thing."

"Well, I have. Got a call from Hugh Everett asking me for permission to test the viability of various wormholes. Except he called them bridges."

"That's what Einstein called them when he first theorized the existence of wormholes in 1935."

"Nineteen thirty-five? Geez, you weren't even around then."

"And you were just a young whippersnapper."

"What's a whippersnapper?"

"Sort of a budding asshole."

"Really?" Lucifer said, obviously hurt.

Mili felt instantly regretful.

"Honey, you're not an asshole anymore."

The Devil eyed Mili warily.

"Anymore?"

"You were quite a handful when I first met you," Mili said.

"And you kept ordering me around," Satan replied. "Do you remember?"

"You required a bit of training."

Lucifer gazed at Mili's face on his monitor.

"If you say so," he responded in a pouty tone.

"There were, of course, other things at which you excelled. And all I could do was watch and admire you."

Mili pointed at her little pregnancy belly.

"Thank you, love. You have allowed me to salvage some of my self-esteem."

"Smooches," Mili said. She puckered her lips and sent her husband some noisy air kisses.

"Will you be coming back to the kibbutz tonight?" Lucifer asked.

"By dinner, I hope."

"The kids need to see you, Mili. And Sriracha will likely have your gift ready for you. Don't tell him I blew his secret."

"Never. One more thing, though. Can we go back to Hugh's request?"

"Sure."

"Did he say where or when he wanted to test the selected bridges?"

"Not precisely," Lucifer answered. "But he did say that Watson had suggested a preliminary location where a modern serial killer had operated without ever being apprehended."

"So, a case like Jack the Ripper's," Mili said. "But why?"

"Everett had instructed Watson to carry out such a location search thinking that, rather than ceasing his murderous activities, Jack may have stumbled onto a time bridge and carried on his dreadful business far away from London where everyone was looking for him. Watson congratulated Hugh on the suggestion, and within moments found a case so much like the Ripper's that he has conjectured that the real Jack the Ripper found a time bridge from London to twenty-first century Long Island, New York, and proceeded to use it multiple times. There is a small localized area on Long Island where a number of murdered women were found, and Hugh is sure that a wormhole is located there as well."

"From the year 1888?" Mili asked and held her breath.

"To and from London, England, August 1888."

"Oh, thank you, love!" Mili cried.

"Watson apparently told Everett quite emphatically that finding Jack the Ripper on the other side of the bridge is virtually one hundred percent certain. He emphasized that the man will be armed and extremely dangerous."

Mili responded to Watson's warning.

"Have Hugh tell Watson that the Ripper will be facing something even more dangerous. Two very pissed off Wickett sisters."

CHAPTER SEVENTEEN

Mili and Mardie sat on padded metal chairs at Albert Einstein's blue Formica kitchen table. Dr. Einstein and Hugh Everett III sat with them, and Hugh was projecting images of the Long Island murder site generated by his Watson on a large monitor. There was a black-and-white photograph of a roadside shoulder beyond which stretched undeveloped countryside. A meadow. Scrub bushes. Norway spruce trees.

"Looks a lot like Hell did a few years ago," Mardie commented.

"Very much so," Hugh agreed. "It's an untended stretch of road where more than eighteen murdered sex workers were found between 1996 and 2013. The women were murdered elsewhere, then dismembered, stuffed into burlap sacks, and dumped there. Police fear that there may yet be more undiscovered victims despite multiple searches by authorities.

"The residents of the area called the serial killer the Craigslist Ripper and the Long Island Ripper. And the similarities to Jack's style *are* striking. The women were prostitutes who advertised their availability on electronic advertising forums. They were used for sex and then murdered. Their heads were severed and their bodies cut into pieces with slashing chops and blows. The police have not released any information about mutilations to the corpses. But sources not authorized to speak about the cases nonetheless described personally witnessing facial and body cuts, punctures, and missing organs."

Hugh looked at Mili.

"Watson thinks that the original Jack the Ripper discovered and used a bridge from his time to ours. Watson concluded that he located it by chance, but figured out how to use it and traveled to the future on many occasions to murder new victims. Watson theorizes that the opening to this time bridge is somewhere near these dumping grounds. I am sure he is right. We can go there and look for it, or we can ask Lucifer to locate it for us."

"Hugh, you've found wormholes on your own many times," Mili said.

Everett nodded.

"Yes, and I could probably calculate the location of this one pretty quickly. But divine beings like your husband can actually sense their presence. Having Lucifer identify it would save us serious effort. Two or three days for sure. A demon—aka a fallen angel—could find it too, but then the presence of this specific time travel corridor would surely be leaked to the smuggling network here in Hell. God knows how many bridges the devils have already found and misused."

Mardie found it very disturbing to think about that. With black market demons able to roam freely through wormholes to fetch whatever was wanted by their well-heeled customers, she had to wonder how many world events had been subject to demonic manipulation purely to satisfy some client's greed. The outbreak of global conflict in the first World War in 1914? The crash of global stock markets in 1929? The robbery of the Bank of England in 1992? Egad. She'd think about this later.

"I will ask Lucifer to help us when I see him tonight," Mili promised.

"And you truly intend to use this bridge, once it's located?" Dr. Einstein asked. His face looked very troubled by the thought.

Mili nodded. Einstein shook his head.

"There is a very important thing for you to consider in making such a decision," Hugh told her. "Watson has only theoretical data about the possible effects of time travel. If Jack the Ripper was able to use it multiple times then there are likely no profound effects. However, Dr. Einstein is concerned that visiting 1888—even only for a brief time—might actually equate to the passing of several days or even several weeks *down here*.

"Jack may well have experienced that kind of time fluctuation as his victims appear to have been murdered over a fifteen year period. Meaning that each time he dispatched a victim, his return to London put him far ahead of the time he had left. It is a possibility that if *you* use the time bridge to go to London, your return here may also put *you* well ahead of the date you left."

That weighed heavily on Mili. Even just a single trip could cause her to lose precious time watching Little Mardie turn into a woman. Or seeing Sriracha grow into a young man. She shook her head. She had no choice but to chase Jack the Ripper through time. But the price might well be painful and personal. And that's if she *wasn't* discovered and killed first by the Ripper himself in merry old England.

※ ※ ※

Mili took a taxi to the kibbutz and had dinner with Lucifer, Little Mardie, and Sriracha. Everyone ate fried trout, red potatoes, corn, green beans, fresh sourdough bread, and fruit preserves. Except for Sriracha. He ate a grilled cheese sandwich and a hefty mound of macaroni and cheese. Mili watched, then finally leaned over to whisper a bit of motherly concern in her son's ear.

"Sweetie, do you know that if you eat too much cheese it can make it hard to go potty?"

Sriracha looked up at Mili.

"Number one or number two?" he asked.

"Number two."

"I don't have any trouble going number two."

"I'm saying that if you eat too much cheese you might *start* to have trouble."

"What do you mean by trouble?"

"You will go number two less often, and it will be more of an effort."

"I'll go less often?" Sriracha's expression was quizzical.

"Yes."

Sriracha rapidly dished several large spoons of macaroni and cheese into his mouth.

"Honey, what are you doing?" Mili said alarmed.

"Eating enough macaroni and cheese to make sure I *never* have to go number two again."

Mili rolled her eyes.

Sriracha grinned and rolled his eyes, too.

"So, darling," Lucifer asked Mili. "You now possess knowledge of a time bridge to London. Are you feeling ready to proceed?"

Mili reached over and squeezed her husband's hand.

"Mardie and I have the exact longitude and latitude for the Long Island portal logged into our GPS. And we'll memorize precisely where the time bridge opens on the London side."

"Have you and Mardie tried your costumes on yet?"

"We have," Mili replied. "I wear a long blue dress and look like a middle-class matron. Mardie is supposed to wear a long red skirt and a white blouse, but she is still campaigning to wear stretch pants and a loose blouse with an elastic top."

"Folks will think that *you're* out for the day," the Devil commented. "And that Mardie is out for the night."

"Displaying her wares."

"*Selling* her wares," Satan amended. "What exactly is your plan?"

"Mardie and I will find the spot where Jack's first murder will occur. He will approach Mary Ann Nichols the night of August 31, 1888, on Buck's Row in Whitechapel. We will be close enough to see his face and bring that identification back to Hell."

Lucifer frowned and stared at Mili.

"I can hardly believe that you and Mardie will just stand by and watch Jack murder that young woman."

"We have no choice."

"Yes, you do," Satan insisted. "You could bring Bobbies to the scene and have Jack arrested for rape."

"You can't rape a whore in 1888, dear boy. By definition, it's a pay-per-use transaction."

"What about having the Metropolitan Police go with you to the location of the *second* murder and catch the bastard then?"

"*That* I could do. But how would I prove it was Jack who murdered the first girl? No witnesses. No photographs. Nothing."

"And what exactly will stop you or Mardie from just shooting the Ripper?"

"It would change history. That is something we will not do," Mili stated resolutely.

"I only wish I could believe you," Lucifer replied. "You and Mardie are passionate women. I just can't imagine either one of you turning away from an opportunity to end Jack's reign of terror."

"I am not going to London to play God," Mili said quietly. "I just want to see the Ripper's face. Then I'll return *here* and play God. So long, Jack the shite."

Sriracha held his hand up.

"What?" Mili asked him, irritated at his interruption.

"Sorry," Sriracha said. "When I hold my hand up, that means I have a question. I learned that in Hebrew school."

"Okay, honey. I'm sorry I was impatient. You can put your hand down now. What is your question?"

"What is shite?"

Mili pointed at his plate.

"It's what you will no longer be able to make in the toilet since you ate all that cheese."

"No more shite for me!" Sriracha cheered.

"Be aware though, dear boy," Mili told him. "That it is a word that you shouldn't use around anyone except your family."

"You mean you and Dad?"

"Yes."

"All right. No more shite! No more shite! No more shite!"

"Sriracha!"

"What?"

"Stop saying shite."

Sriracha frowned.

"But you said I could say it around you and Dad."

Mili turned to the Devil, her eyes appealing for help.

"Don't look at me, darling," Lucifer responded. "His literal mind works exactly like yours."

Mili scowled.

"Shite," she said.

* * *

Lucifer and Mili were in bed. Mili was lying in her husband's arms, her head on his chest.

"Are you okay, love?" Satan asked.

"I am just so damn ready to have this case over," Mili answered softly.

"Are you worried about Mardie?"

"No."

"Concerned about using the time bridge?"

"No."

"Anxious having to deal with Jack the Ripper?"

"No."

"So, what then?"

"I hate the idea of being so far away from you and the kids," Mili confessed. "Miles between us are one thing. But a hundred and thirty-two years separating us is a whole new ball game."

Lucifer held Mili close.

"Wherever you are I will always come for you," he told her. "Even if I have to beg Jehovah to save you, I will do it without a moment's hesitation."

Mili put her hand on Lucifer's cheek.

"Those are wonderful sentiments, my love."

"I mean it. Everyone in Hell knows how much you mean to me. In fact, I just remembered that Trump sent over something for you to take to London."

Satan turned on the bedside lamp and reached for an object on the stand. He handed it to Mili.

"A barrel-over-barrel two shot Derringer with a pearl handle," Mili described it and sighted down the barrel. "Is this the same gun that Trump used to shoot the Ripper?"

"It is. He emphasizes that the range is minimal, so you'll have to have to get off almost a point-blank shot if you want it to be effective."

Mili checked to see if the gun was loaded. Yep. Two chambers, two bullets.

"Double your pleasure, double your fun," she said.

"What?"

"Just remembering an old chewing gum jingle."

"Wrigley, right?" the Devil asked.

"Yes."

"I negotiated endlessly to get William Wrigley down here, but he was already rich and he had a big heart. After he created his holiday beach resort for working men and their families on Catalina Island, I knew I was beat."

"Is that how you know about Catalina wine?"

"Yes," Satan answered. "I've drunk a fair share of it, as well as a boatful of other booze on that island."

"Trying to pounce on Wrigley kin?" Mili teased.

"Not really. Just there to party. A slew of them went to USC and they all majored in drinking."

Mili shook her head.

"Please tell Trump thank you for the pistol. I'll use it only if I must."

"It just occurred to me," Satan said, "that you may have to be on the lookout for Jack on Long Island as well as London."

"Just a travelin' girl," Mili responded lightly.

"*My* travelin' girl," Lucifer responded seriously. "Come back to me, love."

CHAPTER EIGHTEEN

Mili and Mardie walked out of a wormhole from Hell onto Long Island, New York. They stood on the gravel shoulder of an old tarmac two-lane road bordering a large grassy meadow. There was no one driving on the road—which Mili thought fortunate—as the sight of her and Mardie would have drawn curious stares.

They were both wearing long dresses and looked like women who'd taken a wrong turn from the nineteenth century. The Wickett sisters had been preceded to this spot by Lucifer. He had come on his own to test the Long Island wormhole for functionality and locate the precise opening of the nearby time bridge to London, 1888.

"Lu said he tossed breadcrumbs to lead us to the opening," Mili reminded her sister.

"And here they are," Mardie promptly announced.

Satan had placed stones together that read *Hello!* Then he made an arrow pointing the direction they were to walk. No more than a dozen feet farther on was another rock formation that read *Here!*

"Tell me when something disappears," Mardie told Mili, then began reaching her hand in various directions. On the fifth try her hand vanished.

"There!" Mili cried.

Mardie grinned and pulled her hand back.

"Into the breech?" she asked her sister.

Mardie was anxious to enter the portal. She had been able to think of nothing but time travel ever since Albert Einstein told her it was possible. She put a foot into the spot where the time bridge beckoned. Her foot disappeared. She looked at Mili, then walked into the space hole and disappeared. Mili followed right behind her.

They were both through in a single step and found themselves standing on a city street late in the afternoon somewhere in London. A London they did not recognize. The buildings were antique and dilapidated. Three or four story wooden affairs with peeling paint and broken windows covered over with boards. The streets were strewn with garbage. Dislodged cobblestones lay everywhere. And there were a lot of people.

Men and women milled about, dressed in old-fashioned black suits and out-of-fashion dresses. Wearing middle class castoffs from the Salvation Army. The older men wore top hats and the younger men wore derbies or caps. No one seemed busy. Many of the women stood around in groups chatting. Some men were watching a black man playing a tall harp. Others were sitting on steps. Or on the sidewalk. Doing nothing.

"We're back in bloody Hell," Mardie exclaimed.

"Damn straight, we are," Mili agreed. "These are London slums in 1888. No work for the poor. Little food. Not a shred of hope. These folks are wearing the one outfit they own. And it hasn't been washed since the day they put it on. Welcome to Charles Dickens' London."

"We're in the Whitechapel district," Mardie said and pointed at a laundry across the street. The words *Very Clean Chinese Laundry* were painted on a windowfront, and below them, 1928 Dorset Street, Whitechapel. "Looks more like Shitechapel," was Mardie's take. She pointed at piles of feces and pools of urine on the sidewalk and in the gutter. Well, that was at least one break for the ghetto dwellers. All the world was their toilet. Mardie was sure that the people who were forced to live in these circumstances would see no irony in that.

"So," Mili said. "We've entered London on Dorset Street in Whitechapel. Not far from where the Ripper will murder his first victim tonight at dusk. I'll remember that the time bridge opening is straight across from that laundry."

Mili looked at Mardie.

"Ready to go on?" she asked. "Or do you want to use the facilities first?" Mili nodded towards the sidewalk.

Mardie gave her sister an ornery look.

"Lead on," she said. "The sun is beginning to set."

Mili walked down Dorset in the direction of Buck Row. She drew blank disinterested stares from the neighborhood folk. Mardie followed her and received a long whistle from a young man sitting on the sidewalk. Mardie smiled at him and thought just don't look too close, sonny.

Mili watched the sun drop behind a tenement building and kept walking until she came to Buck Row. It was a wide thoroughfare with at least two dozen women dressed in white blouses and long black skirts standing next to the buildings, in the alleys, and even in the street itself. Mili and Mardie took refuge in a small alley.

"Geez, it's dark here," Mardie complained.

"This is the very alley where the Ripper will kill Mary Ann Nichols tonight," Mili replied. "She was probably standing among those prostitutes we just saw. Jack will select her and invite her here. It would be best if we move further up the alley."

They walked on another twenty-five yards. Mili went on to the end of the alley to make sure that it emptied onto a city street and did not finish in a dead end.

"Where did you go?" Mardie asked Mili when she returned.

"I wanted to make sure that we can flee if need be."

"Christ! Creep me out, why don't you?" Mardie said with fear in her voice.

"Just a precaution. If we can't escape from Jack, we will be nothing more than two Jane Does tossed into paupers' graves."

"Don't want that."

Mili shook her head.

"No, we don't want that."

Mili pulled the Derringer out of her brassiere. It was so dark now she could barely make out the small gun in her hand. She knew that it was loaded. And that there was no safety.

"What have you got?" Mardie asked. "I can't see it."

"Do you know what a Derringer is?"

"Two shots of life-ending lead."

"Quite so. Trump insisted that I take it."

"Not exactly a long-distance weapon."

"No, it's not," Mili agreed. "To shoot with any accuracy I'll have to be face-to-face with Jack."

Suddenly both Mili and Mardie heard voices at the entrance to the alley. A man was talking loudly and a woman was laughing. They walked into the alley and came within a few yards of where Mili and Mardie were standing. The couple stopped. The man lit a match to his cigarette and both sisters got a complete and clear view of the villain whom history had never seen—Jack the Ripper.

He was tall and powerfully built. His face square and leathery. The darkly tanned visage of a man who'd led a hard, outdoor life. He was middle-aged with several deep horizontal lines in his forehead and a striking vertical scar that ran from a pronounced widow's peak all the way down to his left eyebrow. His nose was bulbous and swollen. The telltale signs of a lifelong drinker. He wore navy-colored workman's pants, a long sleeve white shirt, and black boots. It was without a doubt the same man who had sat on the park bench in Hell and shot Trump and his vigilantes down.

Strikingly, as pungent as the street odors were, both of the twins could tell he smelled heavily of petroleum oil. It was as though his body and clothes had been soaked in it. His match burned low and the vision of the Ripper, the killer who had so long eluded the London Metropolitan Police, went dark.

The man smoked and there was a murmured conversation between him and the woman. Negotiating a price? After another minute Mili and Mardie heard the rustling of the streetwalker's skirt as she lifted it high.

"No," she told the man.

"Do it," he ordered her.

It sounded like the woman lay down on the cobblestone road. Next were the unmistakable sounds of the man thrusting into the whore, and her loud paid-for moans as he did. It suddenly occurred to Mardie that the man was going to slit the woman's throat just as he climaxed. The thought made her shudder.

Mardie whispered in Mili's ear.

"Shoot him."

Mili pushed her away.

Mardie whispered again.

"We'll find him in Hell. Send him there."

Mili didn't react.

Mardie reached in the dark for Mili's hand and grabbed the Derringer. She walked a half-dozen paces in the near blackness and aimed the little pistol at what she believed was Jack's head. He was grunting with his sexual exertions and the woman beneath him screamed just as Mardie pulled the trigger. The pistol blew up in an explosion of light, exposing two bloody gashes in the woman's neck as a comet of hot metal fragments burst into the back of the Ripper's head. Mardie turned and dashed past Mili.

"Run!" she yelled.

Mili ripped off her boots and ran after Mardie. They exited the alley and doubled back toward Dorset Street. They ran as if their lives depended on it until they reached the time bridge opposite the Chinese laundry. Winded, the twins stopped and gasped for breath. They watched the length of Dorset Street. The Ripper had not followed them.

"Goddamnit," Mardie swore. "What the Hell kind of gun did you bring?"

"One that didn't work."

"Ya think?"

"It happens with old weapons. I had guns blow up twice while I worked at Scotland Yard."

"I thought you were unarmed."

"Not always. Some cases required that I carry a weapon. And I did. In my purse."

"Ever shoot anybody?"

"Can't divulge that, sorry. But if I could, I'd tell you that there were four men over the years who drew on me and didn't live to regret it."

Mardie chewed on that information for a minute. Her twin had shot and killed four men.

"So, why didn't you shoot Jack tonight?" she demanded. "The gun might have worked for you."

"That gun wouldn't have worked for God."

Mili could see Mardie's face in the glow of the gas streetlamp.

"Describe the Ripper for me," she said.

"Why?"

"I want to see if we remember the same beast."

"Smelled like oil," Mardie responded. "And dressed like a workman. Maybe a dockhand who unloads barrels of oil."

"Why would you say that?"

"This day and age is still the era of gas," Mardie elaborated. "Coal gas lights that streetlamp behind you and electricity is just being experimented with in Paris. But petroleum? No one uses petroleum. No one since the Celts who built Stonehenge and rubbed their faces and chests with it. No one around here is going to smell like petroleum unless he is a stevedore unloading it. Or a tradesman using it in who knows what manner.

"The Ripper was tall and muscular and his face was deeply tanned," Mardie continued. "Again, it inclines me to think that he might be a longshoreman who has labored outdoors all his adult life. His face was lined with a long white scar that ran from his scalp to his eyebrow. His nose was large and swollen from drinking to excess. All in all, Jack has a distinct and memorable face."

"Brilliant," Mili told her sister. "We saw exactly the same man, though I didn't observe the damage to his nose. I simply saw it as outsized."

"His nose was completely distended by alcohol-damaged veins swollen beneath the surface tissue."

"My goodness. How did you notice that?" Mili asked.

"I had an affair with a mortician who liked to do it next to the cadavers," Mardie explained. "Saw a lot of chaps who'd bunged up their noses with booze."

"TMDI."

Mardie stared at Mili with a questioning look on her face.

"Too Much Disgusting Information," Mili explained.

"As if you haven't seen the worst shite imaginable," Mardie countered.

"You'll get no argument from me," Mili said. "But I wasn't getting humped when it was staring me in the face."

"Enough of this banter," Mardie said. "Are we out of here?"

"Yes, we are," Mili said. "But we're coming back. Tonight, the Ripper had intercourse with Mary Jane Nichols and then slit her throat. One week from now on September 8, he will kill Annie Chapman on the other side of Whitechapel on Hanbury Street. We're not going to let that murder take place."

"All right," Mardie agreed. "But before I agree to come back, I want a *new* Derringer that shoots flawlessly."

"Done. We'll each have *two*. Plus, extra bullets."

Mardie frowned.

"What for?" she asked.

"In case we need to shoot Jack more than eight times."

Mardie nodded.

"One can only hope."

* * *

Mardie and Mili stepped into the time bridge and returned to New York's Long Island. It was mid-afternoon. Mardie reached down beside a large rock and retrieved her mobile phone from under a pile of leaves and pebbles. It was very dirty. She frowned, brushed it off, and turned it on. The hour matched her expectation. They were five hours earlier than London time. But the date didn't match. She and Mili had left at 3:00 p.m., Friday, August 31. Her mobile read 6:44 p.m., Wednesday, September 5. She looked at Mili who was watching her.

"We lost five days."

"We *invested* five days," Mili corrected her. "With exceptional results. We were eyewitnesses to the Ripper's horrible crime and we can swear on a Bible as to his exact appearance. The real issue with lost days is that we must return to London immediately before Jack murders Mary Chapman in less than forty-eight hours."

"Then what are we waiting for?" Mardie cried. "Let's get home."

Mili pointed in the direction of the wormhole back to Hell. Mardie walked over and found Lucifer's pebble message, *Hello!* She walked straight towards the invisible hole and disappeared. Mili followed her, already planning how to procure Derringers for herself and Mardie. She knew in her heart that both she and her sister were going to shoot Jack dead the next time they saw him.

Stopping outside the wormhole, she remembered a random bit of knowledge about the Hindu religion. That there was supposed to be a proper mantra for every situation in life. Words to give her desires power. Words to bend the future to her will. She stepped into of the wormhole to Hell uttering her choice. "Jack, you are so fucked!"

CHAPTER NINETEEN

Mili led Mardie through a grimy industrial zone adjacent to the commercial docks on London's River Thames. It was near the end of the day, and most of the loading and unloading work on the wooden schooners had been done. The ships sat with their sails pulled tight to their spars, lined up row after row against the piers. Exactly the way the steamships would do after them. Followed by the coal-driven merchant ships that Mili and Mardi witnessed on the river as children.

The wharf was dirtier, smellier, and more foul in appearance than they had observed as youngsters in the 1950's. But not by much. Mili was searching for a small shop that would someday be very famous, owned and run by one Henry Kimber. He was an engineer working to develop and refine what he considered the most important invention of the nineteenth century—the internal combustion engine.

He had not created it. That credit went to the German engineers Gottlieb Daimler and Wilhelm Maybach. Kimber's desire was to significantly increase the size of the engine and make it powerful enough to drive lorries, not just cars. His wife Fanny was pregnant with their first child, a son who would be born in this year of our Lord, 1888.

He would be named Cecil and would inherit his father's passion for engines, adapting them for use in inexpensive sports cars and making automotive history with the founding of the Morris Garage brand. Mili was not searching for engines. She was searching for petroleum users, and her research had led her to Henry Kimber. He purchased more oil than anyone else in London.

Mr. Kimber was outside the back of his shop dipping motor parts into a wooden bucket of cleaning solvent. He was wearing brown pants, a white work shirt, a green leather apron that protected his legs down to his ankles, and black boots that were heavily stained. He smelled sour. Like a bitter detergent. The uncleaned parts sitting on the worktable next to him smelled like oil. Petroleum oil. Kimber was a hawk-faced man with a long nose and blonde hair.

"Good day, sir," Mili addressed him.

"Ladies," Kimber replied politely, surprised that women would be visiting his establishment. He held up a hand as though to stop them in their steps. "Be careful not to touch anything, please. This humble little workshop has chemicals capable of burning, staining, and dissolving Hell itself."

Mardie looked at Mili and grinned.

Henry Kimber thought he was being mocked.

"It may sound amusing, my misses," he said. "But every word is true."

Mili nodded respectfully and spoke up.

"Sir, we are searching for a man who smells of petroleum. And as you probably know better than most individuals, its distinctive smell is a somewhat rare odor in London."

"Aye, that it is," Kimber agreed. "Though mark my words, ladies, we will all live to see petroleum oil dominate the transportation world in the years ahead. Powering every vehicle on our highways, large and small."

"Do you have an assistant, Mr. Kimber?" Mili asked.

"I do. His name is McAllister. He manhandles the barrels of petroleum I import from Pennsylvania. The finest crude available anywhere, by the way. He meets the ships and brings the barrels up here to my shop." Kimber pointed at several large wooden barrels pushed up against a tall fence that shut in his property.

"What is his first name?" Mili asked.

"I don't know," Kimber replied shaking his head. "All he ever told me was that his name was A. McAllister. I didn't ask for more. I employ his strong back and am happy to have the use of it. He's a quiet, respectful man, who keeps track of my shipments, and never fails to deliver them promptly when they arrive at the port."

"What exactly is the petroleum for?" Mili asked.

"I refine it into gasoline and use it to fuel the operating engines. I also use oil in its natural form to lubricate the moving motor components themselves."

"May I ask where Mr. McAllister is now?"

"Don't rightly know, I'm afraid," Kimber replied. "Though he does like to spend time with easy ladies, if you take my meaning."

Mili felt faint. Mardie put her hand over her heart. They'd identified Jack the Ripper.

"Hurry!" Mardie cried running ahead of her sister. Mili paused long enough to rip open the laces on her Victorian boots and yank them off. Her feet didn't like the cobblestones, but she ran like Hell until she caught up with Mardie. The twins ran across the upper north side of Whitechapel, picked up Hanbury Street, and headed towards its terminus at Commercial Road. In an unlit alley near that intersection the Ripper was at that very moment approaching his second victim. Just as Mardie and Mili entered Commercial Road, a terrible scream came from the alley. Both sisters pulled the Derringers out of their bras.

"We're too late!" Mardie cried. She paused beneath a gas lamp. "But he has to exit here!"

No more than five minutes later the man Mili and Mardie recognized as the serial killer Jack the Ripper emerged from the alley buckling his belt. He walked straight toward them. He was wearing blue workman's pants, a long sleeve white denim shirt, black boots, and he smelled like petroleum oil. He was carrying a leather satchel. He saw the women and stopped a dozen feet away. He had no doubt they were waiting for him. It took him a moment to realize that both of the women were pointing pistols at him. He was instantly infuriated. He shook his fist and cried out.

"What do you bleedin' bitches want?" he cried. McAllister had a heavy, central London Cockney accent. "Are you the wenches what shot me in the back of me fuckin' head?"

"We certainly fuckin' are," Mardie hollered back. "And now we're going to shoot you in the *front* of your fuckin' head."

McAllister scowled.

"What?" he yelled outraged.

"We're going to shoot you in the face, moron," Mardie told him.

McAllister pulled a long knife out of his belt and faced the women menacingly.

"What does A stand for?" Mardie shouted.

"Nothing," the Ripper hollered. "Just A."

"I can't believe this conversation," Mili complained.

"*You* talk then," Mardie snapped.

Mili addressed McAllister.

"Your murderous activities are over."

"Cause you're going to shoot me in the face?"

"Yes," Mili replied calmly. "Why did you hurt those women?"

"No reason," McAllister answered. "And every reason. It was easy. It felt good. I do it whenever I want to. And no one can stop me."

"You slit the throats of two young women simply because it was easy?" Mili asked.

"There are a lot more than two."

"Who else?" Mili asked.

"Wouldn't you like to know?" McAllister sneered, then suddenly sprang at Mili knife in hand. She emptied all four barrels of her Derringers. Mardie simultaneously fired her Derringers as well. A. McAllister stopped and stood perfectly still. Then he crumpled to the ground.

"I would have liked to have had those names," Mili said ruefully.

"No problem," Mardie told her. "You're going to get another chance to ask him in Hell."

Mili stared at the body of Jack the Ripper. His face was shot to pieces, but he had also seen *their* faces. Now it was a matter of finding him in the underworld before he found them. And he had a good start. He'd gone to Hell just now, but it was more than a hundred years earlier in time. Which meant that ever since she and Mardie had reunited down in Hell—almost twenty years ago now—he'd already known who they were.

Mardie looked at Mili and began reloading her pistols.

"Let's go, sweetie," Mili urged.

Mardie went with her, but only after emptying both of her Derringers one more time.

※ ※ ※

"Is this him?" Lucifer put down a large black-and-white photograph on his office desk. Mili and Mardie looked at it.

"There's no question," Mili said. "That's the Ripper."

Mardie thought about having shot all of her bullets at that mug. Twice. How had she managed to hit him? She'd never fired a gun before except for the Derringer that had blown up. Maybe she'd been Annie Oakley in another life. No, no, no. Impossible. That homely bitch never got laid. Mardie shook her head. She was thinking about murder, and sex, and shooting all in the same microsecond. Christ. The brain had a mind of its own.

"His admission file says his name is A. McAllister," Satan said. "What does the A stand for?"

"Just A," Mili told him. "Heard it from the man himself."

Lucifer continued.

"His file also says that he was attacked and shot to death in a London alley. The Metropolitan Police believed that McAllister had murdered two prostitutes in the days before he was killed. He had sex with them and cut their throats."

"Yes," Mili responded. "He did."

Satan eyed her for a long moment.

"I thought the Ripper killed *five* women," he said.

Mili shook her head and didn't answer.

"You know that you changed history, don't you?" Lucifer said bluntly.

"We saved the lives of the three women who were Jack's next victims," Mili replied.

Lucifer looked pissed.

"I didn't show you the *other* police photographs. Of McAllister *after* the fact. He'd been shot a dozen times. All in the face."

"By the Wickett sisters," Mardie said proudly. "Let's be clear about that. Point-blank range, and we didn't miss once."

"Twelve Derringer shots to the face?" Satan asked.

"Damn straight," Mili said. "I had two Derringers and so did Mardie. I would have traded mine though for one of those six-shooting revolvers the Ripper used on Trump's vigilantes."

"Trump is not his name anymore," Lucifer said through clenched teeth. "It's *Coogan*. He has no idea that it was ever anything else."

"When did that happen?" Mili asked.

"During the six days you were gone."

Mili frowned. Six days?

The Devil looked at Mardie and then at Mili. Little flames popped up on the top of his head.

"Don't get started, Lu," Mili warned him. "Any changes we caused are probably miniscule."

Flames shot down Lucifer's shoulders and arms.

"Tell that to *President* Coogan," he replied. "My Coogan is *his* son!"

"I thought he was Dorian Gray," Mardie interrupted. "You know. Young and handsome. Evil to the core."

"He lied. He was never Dorian Gray."

"So, who is?"

"*His father!* Keeps saying he's going to make America great again."

"McAllister knows who we are," Mili said changing the subject. "Has ever since we first got here. He knows what we did."

"You mean change history?" Lucifer almost shrieked.

"I mean shooting his face off," Mili answered refusing to acknowledge Satan's hysteria. "He will be stalking us seeking revenge, and the man has some serious Colt revolvers."

"And that's only the hardware he allowed you to see," the Devil told her. "He may have a lot more fire power at his disposal."

"Thanks to the demon black market that *you* allow," Mili shot back.

"Lay off the demons," Lucifer ordered.

"Okay, Mr. Eternal Optimist. Has Trump talked to you about the spy he believes is in your office?"

"No, *Coogan* has not," Lucifer snapped.

"Well, talk to him! He told me that McAllister was in the park *waiting* for him and the vigilantes because someone in your organization—maybe one of your precious demons!—tipped him off!" Flames raced down Satan's arms and danced on the table. "He shot and killed four men because he was *forewarned!*" Mili cried.

"I won't listen to this!" Lucifer hollered.

"You'd better listen!" Mili shouted back. "*Because that same mole is going to set us up next, Lucifer Morningstar!*"

The Devil's flames instantly went out.

"You're right," he said. "I'm sorry, Maggie."

"Maggie?"

"Oops." Satan shook his head. "My bad. I thought your name had been changed, too, because *you* didn't listen to what I said about altering history."

Mili looked at him without responding. Then she raised her fist, fingers curled tight. Then she extended it toward her husband and lifted up her middle finger. Lucifer was instantly offended. Good, Mili thought. Some things haven't changed.

CHAPTER TWENTY

"I need cake balls," Mili told Mardie. "As soon as possible."

"I have two new boxes at home and a cupboard full of chocolate."

"Have I ever said how much I love you?" Mili asked.

"The last time I served you cake balls," Mardie answered.

The twins were sitting on the front steps of Lucifer's office building. Mili was upset, and so was her husband. The sisters had walked out on him after he had picked up a sheet of paper and held it out for them to see.

"Here is a list of the reality changes we've been able to determine *so far* based on your assassination of Jack the Ripper," he had said waving the paper at them.

"Assassination?" Mili mocked. "We squashed a *bug*. Good riddance to that filth."

"Yeah!" Mardie echoed. "And you're pissed off about one lousy page? That's not so bad."

"This page is the first of 1,115,172,016 pages!" the Devil shouted. "Each page contains hundreds of thousands of links to Watson's data banks."

Mardie squinted at the sheet Lucifer was holding.

"I can't read it."

"No, you can't!" Satan told her. "It's printed in nine font reduced to the twentieth power. You need an electron microscope to read it."

"Who has one of those?" Mardie asked mockingly.

"*I* do, Mardie!" Lucifer shouted again. "I had to fucking buy one to read this!"

"We need to call Pfotenhauer," Mardi said sitting on the curb afterwards.

"Lucifer said Pfot was at the kibbutz watching the kids," Mili replied. "Before he went ballistic."

Mili grabbed her phone and punched in Pfotenhauer's mobile number. His face came on the screen when he answered.

"Hello, Mrs. Mili," he said. "I believe a welcome home is in order."

"Thank you, dear boy."

"Lord, we missed you and Miss Mardie," Pfotenhauer continued. "Your last trip took you away from us for days and days."

"Actually, we were only gone for a day, but the price of traveling through time was a basket full of lost days down here. How are you, and how are the children?"

"Little Mardie has lots of friends and has fallen quite hard for that young handsome chap you met."

"Arie Millatiner," Mili remembered. "I liked him. Seemed like a very nice boy. But who knows what he and Little Mardie are up to when no one is watching, eh? Any hanky-panky?"

"Just me I'm afraid."

"You cute thing."

Pfot's face had turned fuchsia.

"Were you ever married on Earth?" Mili asked him.

"No, ma'am. I denied myself that privilege because of my connections with the mob."

"Why did that prevent you from taking a wife?"

"Never knew when the day would dawn that I'd leave a widow behind. Same reason I didn't indulge in the happy task of raising any wee ones."

"I understand, Pfot. Let me say how grateful I am that you watch my children when Lucifer and I are absent."

"You're welcome, Mrs. Mili. How did your search go for Jack the Ripper?"

"We confronted him in London."

"Thank God you're still alive!"

"We are. But he's not. Mardie and I both unloaded Derringers in his face at the scene of one of his murders."

"Did you discover who the monster was?"

"Yes. He was a dock laborer who transported barrels of petroleum oil from the wharf to an automotive shop. The Ripper smelled like oil, Pfot. Head to toe."

"Too bad you didn't have a match."

"Oh," Mili responded imaging that. "How is Sriracha?"

"Doing brilliantly. He hasn't incinerated anything other than a kibbutz cat. And that was not his fault. He reached out to pet the animal and it hissed. Set off some kind of blinkin' reaction and Sriracha fried it. Poor little chap cried all night."

"I'd have cried if it had been a dog."

"Each to their own, ma'am," Pfot said.

"Sorry. Are you a cat lover?"

"No. I hate the disobedient buggers. Give me a dog any day. They love you no matter how you look or act, bless 'em."

"I would guess that your widow friend is very much like that, too, Pfot," Mili responded. "Happiness together can come at any age. But older partners seem more gracious and tolerant of each other. Are you finding that to be true?"

"Couldn't rightly say, ma'am," Pfot answered. "At this stage, Nancy and I are just shagging each other."

Mili was completely embarrassed that she had waxed eloquent about love when Pfot was *just shagging*.

"May I be so bold as to ask what your plans are now, Mrs. Mili?" he asked. "By my calculations, Jack has had a lot of time to prepare to face you and Miss Mardie."

"I know, Pfot. Sad to say we're a bit stalled right now. Lucifer is incensed over the fact that our disposing of the Ripper sent significant ripples through history. I also think he's angry that he has to go see Jehovah and explain. Apparently, the Big Guy is not too fond of that kind of thing."

Pfotenhauer shrugged.

"Who cares?" he said. "What's he going to do? Send Mr. Morningstar to Hell?"

Mili chuckled.

"It would probably be worse for Lu if he got sent to Heaven," she countered.

"Whoa!" Pfotenhauer cried appreciatively. "He'd be bored out of his gourd!"

"Ha!" Mili snorted. "We actually need to track the Ripper down very quickly," she said turning serious. "Given the fact that he knows it was Mardie and me who killed him, he'll come looking for us, won't he?"

"That's a dreadful thought."

"Truly. But we'll find him. We know his name. We know his face. We know his fate."

"He's a dead man twice over."

"From your lips to Trump's ear."

"Begging your pardon, Mrs. Mili?"

"Sorry. I was referring to Lucifer's assistant, *Coogan*. He has a secret group of former law enforcement agents who periodically apprehend certain individuals from Hell's evildoers—and yes, I realize that sounds redundant—punish them for crimes they commit *down here*.

What I will only describe as extremely sadistic treatment, the victim is subjected to pain and bloodletting over several days until he expires."

"Mob did the same stuff," Pfot said. "But was quicker about it. Everyone was in a hurry to get on and do other things."

"Jesus. That sounds callous."

"Maiming and murdering are occupations like any other, ma'am. You do it. You get used to it. You get bored with it."

"Did you experience that, Pfot?" Mili asked.

"No" he answered. "Remember, I was just a driver and a delivery man. Took the chief wherever he wanted to go. And carted the dead bodies to the bog."

"If I may ask a very personal question dear friend, why was your job terminated?"

"You're being kind to ask, thank you, ma'am. Fact is, the job didn't get terminated. I did.

When I turned eighty, the boss told me that I was going to be retired. He had become concerned that I would not be able to drive at high speeds any longer if Bobbies were chasing our ass. The whole thing was done with dignity, and I had no pain or suffering. The only request I had was to receive a cemetery plot rather than a bit of bog, although most of the folks I planted there were decent enough and would have made acceptable neighbors."

"I visited your grave, Pfot," Mili said. "It's on a nice hillside with a very handsome stone."

"Well, that's a cheery report, thanks, Mrs. Mili," Pfot said happily. "Do you happen to remember what was engraved upon the marker?"

"I don't remember dates and such," Mili answered. "But I do remember the epitaph. It was a bit cheeky, but fun. Who wrote it?"

"The boss's wife, Betty Ann. She was always a sweetie to me. What did it say?"

"Here lies our devoted Pfot. Buried him proper. Not a bog nor a float."

"Wonderful!" Pfotenhauer declared, laughing. "'Buried him proper!' What a hoot."

"I'm glad you're pleased," Mili told him.

Pfot nodded happily.

"May we speak a bit more about Coogan?" he asked.

"Of course."

"There has been a hurricane of gossip about him as of late."

"Demon gossip?"

"Of course," Pfot answered. He arched an eyebrow. "Who else?"

"Where do you hook into that kind of noise?" Mili wanted to know.

"At the bowling alley. I take the Master to bowl at his favorite location, Avalon Lanes. While I wait, the demon help drops by with the latest tidbits. Usually it's just melodramatic nonsense. But ever since the trap you set for the Ripper failed, Coogan's role in that boondoggle has wagged a million tongues."

"Coogan barely survived the Ripper's attack, Pfot," Mili reminded him.

"Yes. Everyone knows he was shot, but that he was wearing a bulletproof vest. Now that's a bit odd, if you ask me," Pfotenhauer went on. "Why did he don such a device on that particular evening? None of his men were wearing them." Pfot's eyes narrowed slightly. "Perhaps they were not offered any?"

Mili frowned, but did not interrupt Pfotenhauer.

He went on.

"Demon scuttlebutt also says that Coogan accessed the weapons black market to procure a Derringer. One specially tinkered to blow up when fired."

Mili's heart sank.

"Pfot, that last piece of news is very disturbing. He gave *me* that defective Derringer. Mardie and I were lucky to escape alive after it misfired when Mardie used it. We knew someone was plotting behind

Lucifer's back, and now hearing about the booby-trapped gun, it's obvious that it's Coogan himself. What in the world could have caused him to turn on us?"

Pfotenhauer shook his head.

"People betray friends and causes for every reason imaginable," he answered speaking slowly. "But for Coogan to set up the Master's wife is stunning. No demon has been able to determine what Coogan is up to. But the fallen angels are ferociously loyal to your husband. I can't imagine how furious they will be when they learn that Coogan gave *you* the blow-apart pistol."

"What is most important, dear Pfot," Mili replied, "is that we find out what Coogan is planning *next*. I have to believe that if he was willing to set me up, he must have ambitions to destroy Lucifer as well. My husband must be protected."

"I will make sure the demon network hears your every word, Mrs. Mili."

"Thank you, Pfot. Can you fetch Mardie and me to the kibbutz anytime soon?"

"Yes, ma'am. I can be there in thirty minutes."

"All the way from the kibbutz? That's impossible."

"Not anymore, Mrs. Mili. Mr. Ben-Gurion's work crews have finished repairing and repaving the highway between the kibbutz and the city, and there won't be any trucks this time of day."

"Thank you so much, Pfot. Mardie and I will be waiting outside of Lucifer's headquarters."

"I take it the Master is not coming?"

"Not right now. He got so angry with me he flamed up."

"I've never actually seen him do that," Pfot said. "But I have heard some awesome stories."

"You mean *terrifying* stories."

"Aye. One demon told me that way back when Jehovah himself had the Master stand in the middle of the desert between Sodom and Gomorrah and let it all hang out."

Mili frowned.

"That's a rather inelegant way of referring to the destruction of those sinful towns," she commented. "But I've heard that tale, too."

"Actually, I was trying to be polite," Pfot demurred.

"No need. You always have permission to speak with me anyway that you wish."

Pfotenhauer nodded and tried again.

"I heard that Lucifer stood between those two bugger-infested villages and burned the living shit out of those aunties."

"Permission withdrawn."

"Be there in half an hour, ma'am."

My goodness, Mili thought after Pfot ended the call. She had just learned why no one in their right mind ever honored a request to speak freely except *Star Trek* officers. And what they heard was carefully scripted. Thank God Pfotenhauer hadn't been one of the show's writers.

She sat down by Mardie on the steps of Lucifer's office building.

"Pfot is on the way."

Mardie looked up from her iPhone.

"I just got an email from A. McAllister," she told Mili. "Can you fucking believe it?"

"I am starting to believe just about anything."

Mardie read it out loud.

"You killed me once. You won't kill me twice. Look around you all the time, Mardie Wickett. I'm coming for you, bitch."

"And Hell used to be such a nice place," Mili said. "Don't let that worry you, Sis. It's posturing bullshit."

Sure, Mardie thought. That's all it is. She carefully looked around. Probably weren't too many things worse though than being killed by posturing bullshit.

CHAPTER TWENTY-ONE

Lucifer ran out of his office, knelt in front of Mili, and took her hand.

"I am so sorry, love," he pleaded. "I never want to be angry with you."

"But you are," Mili reminded him.

"No, I'm not," the Devil protested. "You have to believe me. Pfotenhauer just called me and said a group of demons have located McAllister in an apartment building behind the park where he killed Coogan's men. They have evacuated the area, and he is alone in the building."

"Pfot called *you?*" Mili asked nonplussed.

"He only called me instead of you because he wanted me to starting mobilizing help to take the Ripper down. He asked me to tell you that he is networking while he's on his way over here, trying to find out more about Coogan."

Mili looked into her husband's eyes. Despite all the truly hurtful things said about him over the ages, he really was kind and trusting.

"Darling, listen to me carefully," she told him. "Pfot says that the demons are sure that it was Coogan himself who tipped off the Ripper before the vigilante raid."

"Well, he can't protect McAllister any longer. It's over. I'll have demons tear the Ripper limb from limb if he tries to exit the building."

"What if he surrenders?" Mili asked.

"Then they'll tear him limb from limb *after* he exits the building."

"And if he refuses to leave?"

"We'll burn the building down," Satan answered.

"No mercy?"

"No mercy," the Devil said angrily. "Not for him."

"Wow," Mili replied impressed with Lucifer's resolve. "You're tougher than God."

"Damn straight, I am. Mr. Call-Me-A.-McAllister is going down hard."

Mili watched her husband for a moment, then revealed the last terrible truth about Coogan.

"The demons also told Pfot that Coogan used the black market to get a rigged Derringer designed to blow up when I shot it."

Lucifer was shocked.

"He tried to kill you?" he cried dismayed and furious.

Mili nodded.

"I am convinced that his plan was to get rid of me and then to murder you."

"Well, son of a bitch," the Devil hissed. "That was a big mistake on his part."

"Thinking he could kill you?" Mili asked.

Satan shook his head.

"No. Thinking he could mess with the Wickett sisters."

✳ ✳ ✳

In the heat of the noonday sun, Mili and Mardie stood across the park from the apartment building where A. McAllister was trapped. Lucifer stood next to them. A dozen Samn demons stood nearby. There were additional Samns watching the front and back exits of the property, holding kerosene lanterns they were prepared to toss into the apartment lobby and set the building on fire.

None of them was armed. The Samns could easily tear McAllister apart if given the chance to do so. Mili and Mardi were carrying their Derringers. More for comfort than any real belief they would need to use them. Jack the Ripper was about to pay the price for murdering women in London, Long Island, and Hell. Good riddance.

Mili's attention was drawn to the roof. McAllister appeared on top of the four-story apartment building and stood staring down at them. She called out to him.

"It's the end of the road for you, Jack!"

"I fancy it is, Mrs. Morningstar," he called back with disdain in his voice. "I regret that the tables have been turned on me instead of on *you*, but such is Hell."

"We also know that you recruited Coogan to betray my husband," Mili cried.

"You're wrong on that bit, Missie," McAllister declared. "Long before you ever came looking for yours truly, Coogan hired me to kill you and Lucifer."

Mardie was stunned by McAllister's admission.

"What did he promise you in return?"

"Total freedom to roam anywhere in Hell, doing anything I wanted after you and the Master were disposed of. Probably a lie. Bastard double crossed me and shot me in the park."

Mili shook her head. Poor Lucifer. Betrayed by his closest aide. She looked at her husband. He had a stone face, but his heart was breaking, she just knew. She called out to Jack the Ripper again.

"You have ninety seconds to come down the four flights of stairs inside your building, walk outside, and surrender."

"Alas," McAllister called back. "I cannot comply with your request. One way or another, I know that I will not leave this panoramic perch alive. My only regret is that I did not have the chance to slit your throat and that of your sister."

Mardie stepped forward and shouted at the Ripper.

"The A in A. McAllister stands for *Asshole*, you jerk-off! I hope that's your last conscious thought."

McAllister reached down and then stood up straight again. Before anyone could react, he put the scope of a long-barreled carbine to his eye and aimed at Mardie. The air cracked with the blast of the only shot Jack the Ripper would get off. His bullet hit Mardie in the sternum, shattering it and ripping her heart to pieces. She dropped to the ground dead. The A stands for Asshole was *her* last thought.

✳ ✳ ✳

Mardie woke up in her bed. She was home. She was alive. Again. She was not terribly surprised since Lucifer had both the obligation—and hopefully in her case the desire—to restore her to life with a new Hellion body. Mili was sitting on the edge of the bed holding her hand. Little Mardie was beside her and Lucifer stood at the foot of the bed next to Sriracha who looked distinctly taller than she remembered. The Devil was holding a small boy in his arms. Maybe three years old.

"How long have I been gone?" Mardie asked.

"Almost four years," Lucifer answered. "I'm so sorry. Jehovah refused to grant me an audience after the changes that resulted from Jack the Ripper's death in London. But angels in Heaven interceded for me, and finally the Old Man gave me a presentation slot."

"There are angels in Heaven who *like* you?" Mardie couldn't help but ask.

"I didn't say they liked me," Satan clarified. "Having been created by the divinely good Elohim, they still believe in fairness. Even usurping Jehovah can't change that in them. Anyway, you're back now. I'm sorry it took so long."

"I am grateful. Thank you, Lucifer." Mardie choked up and started to cry. "How much have I missed?"

"A. McAllister was burned to ash in the apartment building fire," Satan answered. "Coogan was apprehended and handed over to the secret organization of ex-law enforcement officers that he once led." Lucifer allowed himself a little smirk. "Never heard another word about him.

"The Morningstar family has become full-time residents at the kibbutz," he continued. "Those industrious folks have recovered another half million acres of Hell's landscape and repaved every road and sidewalk down here. Ben-Gurion and his wife renewed their wedding vows. Moshe Dayan was engaged for a while, but recovered his wits and broke it off. And our beloved Pfotenhauer is enjoying the benefits of a long-term relationship with his widow friend at the kibbutz, Nancy, who introduced him to Viagra.

"I'll let Mili and the kids fill you in on everything, but I do want to tell you that Little Mardie has converted to Judaism and hopes to marry her wonderful Arie soon. Sriracha prefers to speak Hebrew and has an army of little friends at the kibbutz. And while you were gone, Mili gave birth to the kindest, gentlest child anyone has ever met." He kissed the boy he was holding on the cheek. "I don't think he has a flame in his body."

As if on cue, Lucifer's son smiled beatifically. His skin was white as snow and he had long, copper-colored hair that had never been cut. Little Mardie had persuaded Mili to let her give him a special do. A headful of cornrows. He smiled like a saint. He looked like a rock star.

"What's his name?" Mardie asked, sitting up. "Lucifer Junior?"

"Oh my, no," Satan replied. "We didn't want to jinx the kid. We named him Jesus. Jesus Morningstar."

At that, little Jesus clapped his hands and Mardie's bedroom shone with pure Heavenly light.

Mili leaned down and hugged Mardie.

"Welcome back," she whispered, tears filling her eyes. "What's one Wickett sister without the other?"

"I don't ever want it to happen again," Mardie answered.

Everyone climbed on top of Mardie's bed hugging and kissing her. It would take a long time for her to catch up on all the affection she had missed.

"Bring on all that sugar!" she cried happily.

And they did.

Epilogue I

Bowles spent the night with Mardie soon after her return. He was amazed that Lucifer had managed to talk God into giving her a youthful face and body just like he had done years ago with Mili. Not only was Mardie gorgeous, her skin was blemish free and baby-bottom smooth.

"Did you look like this when you were a lass on Earth?" he asked.

"Mostly," she said. "Are you all right with the changes?"

"I am," he answered shyly. "But I was already very happy with the woman I had fallen in love with."

Mardie's eyes grew large.

"I realized it when I lost you, darling," Bowles told her. "I am so sorry I didn't know it or say it earlier."

Happy tears flooded Mardie's eyes.

"No one who spent time with me ever told me that, Bowles."

"Then it's entirely overdue," Bowles said and kissed Mardie tenderly on the lips. "I love you."

"And I love you, my dear Bowles."

"Is this what they call a happy ending?" he whispered in Mardie's ear.

"No," she whispered back. "It's what they call a happy beginning."

Epilogue II

Moshe Dayan had drawn the short straw with Ben-Gurion and thus was watching Lucifer's kids while the Devil and Mili spent the day in the city. He was excitedly cleaning an object he had recovered this very morning at the Mormon archaeological dig site next to the kibbutz. He was stupefied to be looking at what appeared to be an identical set of golden tablets to the ones revealed to Joseph Smith.

They were actually thin sheets of gold, the size and weight of thick pieces of paper, punched with three holes and bound with golden rings. Each page was completely covered with what he instantly recognized as the ancient Linear B script the Myceneans used. Had some of the surviving members of the ten lost tribes of Israel traversed Greece on their way to MesoAmerica?

It wasn't any more farfetched than believing that they had made it all the way to upstate New York. Or down here to Hell. Holy Moroni, Dayan thought. If this was truly *The Book of Mormon* it was the only known copy in existence.

He grinned at little Sriracha who'd been watching him. Then he stuck a cigarette in his mouth. Suddenly a blast of fire emanated from Sriracha's finger as he tried to light Dayan's smoke. He missed and hit the tablets. In a triumphant demonstration of the thermodynamic law of cause and effect the golden sheets were blasted into golden flakes.

Dayan stared at the bits floating in the air, then looked down at Sriracha. Lucifer's son shot another blast of fire and this time lighted Moshe's cigarette. Dayan inhaled deeply. No one had seen the golden *Book of Mormon* except him, and he certainly wasn't going to walk around like Joseph Smith had done, telling everyone about golden tablets he no longer possessed.

He looked at Sriracha.

"Come here kid," he said. "And give me a hug."

The End

Acknowledgments

I would like to thank Mili and Mardie Wickett's faithful friends who have followed their continuing adventures in Hell.

Particularly Dennis Bertacchi, Valorie Carroll, Margie Cleland, Helen Fehr, Peter Haggard, Bobette Jones, Cheri Klein, Michelle Madison, Cynthia Marshall, Liliane Novak, Callie Oakes, Sheridan Oakes, Lorraine Petrakis, and Carolyn Walker, all of whom read and encouraged me on this and other tales about the Wickett sisters.

I want to thank Vincent Chong, yet again, for his cover design and art; Jerry Sexton for his copy editing; Mark Meyer for the final wrap-up at Professional Book Proofreading; WzW for final print formatting; and Lionel Blanchard, my publisher.

www.ingramcontent.com/pod-product-compliance
Lightning Source LLC
Chambersburg PA
CBHW070558010526
44118CB00012B/1369